THE ART OF FLOW

HOW TO GET IN THE ZONE, MAINTAIN RAZOR-SHARP FOCUS, AND IMPROVE YOUR PRODUCTIVITY AND PERFORMANCE AT WILL!

DAMON ZAHARIADES

ARTOFPRODUCTIVITY.COM

Copyright © 2023 by Damon Zahariades

All rights reserved. No part of this publication may be reproduced, distributed, or transmitted in any form or by any means, including photocopying, recording, or other electronic or mechanical methods, without the prior written permission of the publisher, except in the case of brief quotations embodied in critical reviews and certain other noncommercial uses permitted by copyright law. For permission requests, contact the author through the website below.

Art Of Productivity

http://www.artofproductivity.com

CONTENTS

Other Books by Damon Zahariades — vii

Your Free Gift — 1
Notable Quotables about Finding Flow — 3
Introduction — 5
What You'll Learn in the Art of Finding FLOW — 8

PART I
WHAT IS FLOW?

The Essence of Flow — 15
The 7 Life-Changing Benefits of Achieving Flow — 19
The Practical Usefulness of Flow in Every Area of Your Life — 25

PART II
PREPARING TO ACHIEVE FLOW

Laying the Foundation — 35
How Fear Impedes Flow — 39
The Many Triggers of Flow — 44
The Most Formidable Enemies of Flow — 50

PART III
10 STEPS TO ACHIEVING A FLOW STATE

Step #1: Develop and Follow a Pre-flow Routine — 67
Step #2: Identify Your Peak Energy Times — 71
Step #3: Create a Distraction-Free Environment — 78
Step #4: Define a Clear Mission — 83
Step #5: Establish Your Intrinsic Motivation — 88

Step #6: Commit to Monotasking 93
Step #7: Choose a Challenging (But Achievable) Task 99
Step #8: Make Sure You're Rested, Relaxed, and Alert 104
Step #9: Use the Flowtime Technique 109
Step #10: Create a Feedback Loop 115
Solving the Flow Puzzle: A 60-Second Recap 119

PART IV
GREATER AWARENESS ABOUT YOUR FLOW STATE

7 Signs You Have Achieved a Flow State 125
Microflow vs. Macro Flow 132
How to Lengthen a Flow State 135
The Potential Dark Side of Achieving Flow 142

PART V
BONUS SECTION: 10 SIMPLE ACTIVITIES TO PRACTICE GETTING INTO FLOW

Activity #1: Read Long-Form, Non-fiction Content Slowly 149
Activity #2: Brainstorm an Out-Of-The-Box Solution to an Existing Problem 152
Activity #3: Practice a Breathing Routine to Sharpen Your Focus 156
Activity #4: Meditate for 10 Minutes 160
Activity #5: Conduct an Active Listening Session 163
Activity #6: Perform a Mindfulness Drill 166
Activity #7: Do Your Favorite Physical Activity with Hyperfocus 170
Activity #8: Enjoy a One-Hour Digital Detox 173

Activity #9: Question Yourself to Identify Flow Blockages	177
Activity #10: Summarize Content That You Have Read	180
Final Thoughts on the Art of Finding FLOW	183
Did You Enjoy Reading The Art of Finding FLOW?	185
About the Author	187
Other Books by Damon Zahariades	189

OTHER BOOKS BY DAMON ZAHARIADES

The Mental Toughness Handbook

The Procrastination Cure

To-Do List Formula

The Time Management Solution

80/20 Your Life!

The Time Chunking Method

How to Make Better Decisions

The Art of Living Well series

The Art Of Saying NO

The Art of Letting GO

The Art of Finding FLOW

The 30-Day Productivity Boost series

The 30-Day Productivity Plan - VOLUME I

The 30-Day Productivity Plan - VOLUME II

Self-Help Books for Busy People series

Small Habits Revolution

The Joy Of Imperfection

The P.R.I.M.E.R. Goal Setting Method

Improve Your Focus and Mental Discipline series

Fast Focus

Morning Makeover

Digital Detox

Visit ArtofProductivity.com for a complete list of titles and summaries. All titles are available for purchase at ArtofProductivity.com/Amazon.

YOUR FREE GIFT

~

I want to give you a gift to say thanks for purchasing this book. It's my 40-page PDF action guide titled *Catapult Your Productivity! The Top 10 Habits You Must Develop to Get More Things Done.*

It's short enough to read quickly but meaty enough to offer actionable advice that can make a real difference in your life.

You can get immediate access to *Catapult Your Productivity* by clicking the link below and joining my mailing list:

http://artofproductivity.com/free-gift/

In the following pages, you'll learn how to induce a flow state of mind at any time that suits you. We'll explore the entire process together, step by step. By the time you reach the bonus section, you'll have all the tools you need to trigger flow at will. When you're in a flow state, you'll do your most creative and productive work and experience peak performance.

If you're ready, let's dive in.

NOTABLE QUOTABLES ABOUT FINDING FLOW

∼

> The happiest people spend much time in a state of flow – the state in which people are so involved in an activity that nothing else seems to matter; the experience itself is so enjoyable that people will do it even at great cost, for the sheer sake of doing it.
>
> — MIHÁLY CSÍKSZENTMIHÁLYI

> There is an ecstasy that marks the summit of life, and beyond which life cannot rise. And such is the paradox of living, this ecstasy comes when one is most alive, and it comes as a complete forgetfulness that one is alive.

— JACK LONDON, *CALL OF THE WILD* (1903)

> This is the real secret of life — to be completely engaged with what you are doing in the here and now. And instead of calling it work, realize it is play.

— ALAN WATTS

INTRODUCTION

∼

You know the feeling. You've no doubt experienced it more than once. When it happens, it feels almost magical. Surreal, even. And it can seem like something vital is missing when it doesn't happen.

I am, of course, referring to the feeling of working in a flow state. Everything else fades away when you're immersed in whatever you're doing. Your attentional resources are zeroed in upon the task at hand. You become hyper-focused.

Most people believe that a flow state is a product of luck. It occurs when their muse visits them. They assume it's something over which they have no control.

But that's incorrect. We can control numerous factors that allow us to achieve a flow state virtually at will.

But we'll get to that later.

I was introduced to flow when I was a kid. Back then, I swam competitively. For reasons still unclear, my coaches designated me the "long-distance guy," putting me in events such as the 1,500-meter freestyle. The training involved workouts that lasted hours.

Flow rarely happens when you compete in short events (e.g., the 50-meter freestyle). There's no time. You blink, and the event is over. In lengthy events, however, something strange happens. The anxieties of the moment ("Is my rival keeping pace," "I must hit this turn perfectly," etc.) fade away. In its place is a kind of peacefulness. You enter "the zone," where every aspect of your performance break downs into its simplest form.

Stroke. Kick. Breathe.

Even though you're exhausted and your muscles and lungs are screaming for relief, these actions seem easy. You're in complete control, which gives you a feeling of satisfaction. Enjoyable, even.

Since that period, I've enjoyed working in a flow state over and over. I experienced it repeatedly while playing guitar, practicing and "jamming" with bandmates (I was in a garage band). I experienced it in corporate America while reviewing spreadsheets. And today, I often work "in the zone" while writing.

Here's the thing: I learned not to leave this to luck. I learned not to wait for my muse. Instead, I figured out a way to achieve a flow state at will.

This brings us to the purpose of this book. I'll show

you how to achieve a flow state in the following pages. Rather than leaving it to fate or your muse, you'll learn how to get into the zone whenever it suits you. Once you can do this, you'll reap benefits that may seem implausible now.

But we'll get to that later, too.

Let's look at what you'll find in *The Art of Finding FLOW*.

Damon Zahariades
Art of Productivity
May 2023

WHAT YOU'LL LEARN IN THE ART OF FINDING FLOW

∼

This book has a single overriding aim: to train you to achieve a flow state whenever desired. There are two approaches to accomplishing that goal. One involves plunging into the psychology of flow. This includes investigating how the brain works and developing a theoretical framework that supports our proposed methodologies.

The second approach is to focus primarily on the practical aspects of flow. This includes examining how it works in the real world and exploring the steps needed to achieve it.

I strongly favor this latter approach. If you prefer the former method, psychologist Mihaly Csikszentmihalyi (the "father" of flow psychology) has written several remarkably meticulous books on the subject.

You'll notice that *The Art of Finding FLOW* is a short book. That's by design. Every section is written to be immediately actionable or to support sections that are so. There's no fluff. That's the type of self-improvement book I enjoy reading, and I hope you do, too.

Here's a quick roadmap detailing what you'll find in the following pages.

Part I

We'll cover a few essential building blocks of achieving and using flow. To fully appreciate how flow can change our lives, we must first understand what it is.

In *Part I: What Is Flow?* we'll break down this positive psychological state into its simplest components. We'll scrub away the vapid claptrap that usually surrounds it and examine its essence. We'll explore the benefits of working in a flow state and discuss how we can use it in various aspects of our lives.

Part II

This is where the practical part of the training begins. Similar to how a mechanic must understand how a vehicle's components work together to affect its overall performance, we must understand how the many facets of flow do likewise.

In *Part II: Preparing to Achieve Flow*, we'll talk about the effects of fear and how it can prevent you from getting "in the zone." We'll explore circumstances that act as triggers to flow and how you can manage them. We'll also discuss things that'll hamper your ability to achieve a flow state, so you'll be prepared to head them off before they cause problems.

Part III

This is the "how to" part of the book. We'll roll up our sleeves and develop a system for getting into the zone.

In *Part III: 10 Steps to Achieving a Flow State*, you'll learn a reliable method for triggering a flow state and taking full advantage of it. Each step is explained concisely and accompanied by a simple exercise. You may feel inspired to take notes and return to this section for a refresher.

Part IV

The more we know about being in a flow state, the more effectively we'll be able to take advantage of it. Like a chef who fully appreciates the ingredients at his disposal, we'll expand our awareness of flow regarding our experience with it.

In *Part IV: Greater Awareness about Your Flow State*, we'll discuss how to tell when you're in the zone. We'll also talk about remaining in this state when it suits you. Finally, we'll explore the dark side of flow so you'll be fully prepared to prevent troublesome (and often overlooked) issues.

Bonus Section

Training ourselves to achieve flow at will is similar to training ourselves to perform any task successfully. Performing specific activities can hone our mindset. It can help us to create routines that work for us. Like an athlete trains to build endurance and increase strength, we can train ourselves to enter a flow state. When the time comes to do so, this training will streamline the process.

The last section of *The Art of Finding FLOW* will take you through 10 simple exercises. You can do them at any time that suits you. As with *Part III*, you may feel inspired to return to this section repeatedly.

The Road Forward

We have a lot to cover in the following pages. But I promise we'll cover it quickly so you can apply the information soon. Remember, this book aims to train you to get into the zone whenever desired. It prioritizes taking purposeful action to that end.

One final note before we start: I strongly encourage you to perform the exercises you'll find throughout this book. They're simple, easy, and take little time (time estimates are provided for each one so you can plan them around your schedule).

The exercises continue to help me, and I feel they'll help you, too.

Onward.

PART I
WHAT IS FLOW?

∽

Achieving flow is commonly misunderstood to be a strategy to increase productivity. This misconception prevents people from enjoying its full range of benefits. While working in a flow state can make you more productive, the boost in productivity is merely a byproduct. It's not the main reason to achieve flow.

The main reason to work in a flow state is that it makes us feel more engaged with whatever we do. When we're fully engaged, we feel more fulfilled. More satisfied. Happier.

These positive feelings enrich our daily experience in ways that many people overlook. Our lives feel more meaningful. Our decisions and actions feel more purposeful and consequential. We enjoy a greater sense of ownership, empowerment, and personal agency.

Ultimately, these feelings can inspire us to accomplish remarkable things in our lives — and, importantly, to do so with more joy and gratification.

THE ESSENCE OF FLOW

∼

At its simplest, flow is a state of total mental absorption. Our entire inventory of attentional resources is zeroed in on our current activity. Whatever we're doing, we're doing it with complete immersion and at peak performance.

Athletes have described flow as a state where they feel calm and energized, even as their bodies are under great stress. Students describe flow as becoming hyperaware of the subject matter they're studying while losing awareness of their environment. Artists describe flow as an almost trance-like state where they can create art effortlessly and without inhibition.

But this doesn't mean that working in a flow state is easy. We often experience the best results when we push ourselves to the limits of our abilities and tolerance for discomfort.

Flow Requires a Challenge

The positive feelings from working in a flow state stem from overcoming a challenging task. If a task is easy, accomplishing it won't feel rewarding beyond crossing it off our to-do list. If it's undemanding, it's unlikely to engage us.

People who regularly achieve flow report that they feel most engaged when doing something difficult for them. For example, athletes in the zone push their bodies to the limits of their endurance. Students struggle as they mentally grasp and master complex concepts. Artists wrestle with their inner critics, fighting to silence them.

It's in the midst of these challenging circumstances that a flow state becomes attainable. The difficulty involved in whatever we're doing increases our absorption and sharpens our focus to the point that everything else fades into the background. The upside is that we'll likely feel a greater sense of engagement once we induce flow.

The Sweet Spot of Flow

It's not enough to be confronted with a challenge. We must also possess the requisite skills needed to rise to it. Moreover, our skill set should be in balance *with* the challenge.

If we lack the skills needed to meet the challenge, we're

likely to feel stressed and frustrated. On the other hand, if we think that we possess skills that greatly exceed the challenge, we're likely to feel bored. Neither of these feelings is conducive to working in a flow state.

When there's a proper balance between our skills and the task that interests us, we simultaneously experience a sense of control and stimulation. We feel that we're up to the challenge rather than feeling anxious or apathetic. We're excited — inspired, even — to roll up our sleeves and tackle the task.

Flow vs. Hyperfocus

Before we move on, we must distinguish working in a flow state from hyperfocus. The two are often conflated, and it's worthwhile to recognize their differences.

We've already described flow. We've discussed what it is and how it feels to work in this state of consciousness. It's a desired state that can be triggered and harnessed to benefit us.

Hyperfocus is different. It typically stems from an inability to manage attentional resources. A person who experiences hyperfocus is consumed by whatever task holds their attention. For example, a child may be so spellbound by a video game that they can't hear people calling their name. An adult might be so fixated on a home-improvement project that they forget meals and miss appointments. This might seem similar to flow but is associated with impulsiveness and a lack of emotional control.

Hyperfocus is often discussed in the context of attention-deficit/hyperactivity disorder (ADHD). While it may share some attributes with flow on the surface, its underlying triggers differ. Most importantly, hyperfocus can pose adverse effects that have severe consequences if left unmanaged.

This book focuses on flow, including achieving and making the most of it. To that end, we'll abandon the subject of hyperfocus here.

THE 7 LIFE-CHANGING BENEFITS OF ACHIEVING FLOW

∼

As mentioned, we often think of working in flow as a means of being more productive. We'll get more done if we're so focused on our work that we're completely immersed and engaged.

This is true to some degree. But we can harness myriad other rewards by working in a flow state. If we fixate on increased productivity, we risk overlooking these other perks.

Here are seven reasons to learn how to trigger this positive mental state to fully appreciate everything we stand to gain.

Benefit #1: Greater Creativity

Two of the most common obstacles to creativity are fear and self-consciousness. Whether we're trying to paint a landscape, write a novel, or come up with out-of-the-box solutions to a problem at work, we worry about our output. Will it be good? Will it meet others' expectations? Will it meet *our* expectations? Can we do better?

When we're in the zone, we're less fearful and self-conscious. We're less anxious about our results because we focus on the creative experience.

Benefit #2: Immunity to Distractions

We're susceptible to internal and external distractions whenever we work on a task that fails to interest us and captivate our attention. Internal distractions include everything in our heads, such as self-doubt and mind wandering. External distractions include anything in our immediate environment, such as social media, our phones, and our coworkers' conversations.

When we work in a flow state, these distractions fade away. They're still present, but we no longer notice them. We're no longer aware of them and thus susceptible to them.

Benefit #3: Faster Learning and Mastery

Most of us aspire to be faster learners. Picking things up quickly makes us more adaptable to our circumstances, more marketable to potential employers, more interesting to our friends, and more satisfied with our newfound knowledge and skills. The problem is that learning new things quickly is a struggle for many of us. And mastery can sometimes seem impossible.

Working in flow accelerates learning. While in a flow state, we're no longer hindered by distractions, frustration, anxiety, and self-doubt. Instead, we're excited to learn the subject in front of us. We're fully attentive to it as everything else fades into the background.

Moreover, as we learn this new knowledge or skill, we experience a positive feedback loop. The better our grasp of the subject, the more satisfied, confident, and happier we feel. These feelings, in turn, motivate us to continue until we've mastered the issue.

Benefit #4: Heightened Sense of Happiness

Happiness has many definitions. But at its core, it's understood to be an emotional state characterized by joy and satisfaction. When we're happy, we feel fulfilled and content.

It's not a fixed state. Our happiness fluctuates with our circumstances, expectations, and our emotional responses.

But we'll be happier if our needs are met and we do things that align with our interests.

Working in a flow state elevates this feeling. We can tackle the challenge in front of us without anxiety and feel accomplished and satisfied as we work. We enjoy what we're doing because it aligns with our interests. And importantly, we don't feel pressured or self-conscious while doing it. In this state, our inner critic and other internal and external distractions are made silent.

Benefit #5: Positive Stress

Emotional stress is commonly thought to be a negative response to our circumstances. The demands placed upon us cause us to feel pressured, alarmed, and even fearful. Everyone experiences periods during which they feel stressed.

Because of these negative implications, most people try to minimize their stress. But stress isn't always bad. It doesn't always hurt us. Stress can be highly beneficial in select circumstances.

When we achieve flow, we often experience something called *eustress*. This is a form of stress that energizes us. When we confront stressors, we feel confident that we can overcome them. The pressure to perform is present, but rather than feeling anxious, we feel self-assured in our abilities.

Benefit #6: Emotional Control

All of us occasionally lose control over our emotions. We get angry when a driver cuts us off during our morning commute. We feel frustrated when a coworker fails to pull their weight. We feel dispirited when life burdens us with one fiasco after another.

There's no shame in admitting that our emotions get away from us now and then. But we can learn to regulate them, and working in a flow state can help us do so.

We feel focused, confident, and engaged in the zone. Rather than feeling like powerless victims of our circumstances, we trust our ability to cope, respond rationally and purposefully, and overcome.

Benefit #7: Increased Productivity

I noted above that working in flow offers us much more than just a boost in productivity, and I discouraged fixating on this particular benefit. But it would be silly to ignore it. The fact is that research shows we're far more productive when we work in this state.[1]

The reasons are clear. When we experience positive emotions related to our actions, we perform better. We're happier, more confident, more creative, and more purposeful. This allows us to work more effectively and, ultimately, more productively.

I'm not referring to the kind of productivity that pushes you to cross off dozens of items from your to-do list in record time. Instead, I'm talking about the kind where you're accomplishing something important to you. You're achieving something that aligns with your goals.

Are You Willing to Go with the Flow?

There's a lot at stake. You stand to reap lifelong, transformative rewards by consistently learning to work in a flow state. Will you pursue this and learn to do so?

At this moment, you may think that working in flow only applies to athletes, creatives, and select career paths. But that's incorrect. The reality is that you can benefit from getting in the zone in every aspect of your life.

---

1. *Increasing the 'meaning quotient' of work.* (2013, January 1). McKinsey & Company. https://www.mckinsey.com/capabilities/people-and-organizational-performance/our-insights/increasing-the-meaning-quotient-of-work

THE PRACTICAL USEFULNESS OF FLOW IN EVERY AREA OF YOUR LIFE

∽

You can take advantage of working in flow whenever you're doing something that requires you to focus. This includes activities at work, at home, in class, and even during your free time.

At work, being in the zone can benefit you whether you're a farmer, physician, plumber, or architect. You can make good use of it at home whether you're doing chores, studying, or meditating. You might be in the zone during your free time while you garden, read, or cook.

The point is that you can work in a flow state of mind while doing myriad activities, some of which may not be evident. Let's explore a few of them below.

Flow While Working

No matter your profession, you're vulnerable to distractions. Your ability to focus and remain effective is always at risk, threatened by your environment.

For example, you probably contend with chatty coworkers if you work in an office. If you work in a hospital, phones, patients, and computerized alerts might wreak havoc with your ability to focus. If you're a lawyer, emails and texts from clients can make it difficult for you to concentrate. If you're a software engineer, you're always one click away from the internet, a bottomless rabbit hole of distractions.

You can create a flow experience at your job no matter what that job is. When you do, you can keep distractions at bay and focus on your work. You'll become more productive and more effective, and you'll feel more engaged in the process.

Flow at Home

Think about the activities you do while you're at home. Here are a few examples:

- Household chores
- Exercise
- Study
- Meditation
- Work on home improvement projects

- Learn a new skill
- Journal
- Build a side business

You can do each of these activities while you're in the zone. When you do, you'll enjoy doing them more — even your household chores. You'll feel more aware, attentive, and energized.

Flow While Creating

Creating something new can be a deeply gratifying experience. Many positive emotions accompany the act of doing so. When you successfully create something, your brain is flooded with dopamine, the "feel-good" chemical.

What types of things might you create? Here's a quick list:

- A song on your guitar or piano
- A painting you've envisioned
- A novel you've dreamed of writing
- A new product for your side business
- An inspired gift for a friend
- A new dish based on an original recipe
- A clever game for your children to play

The creative process is easier when you're in a flow state of mind. There are fewer barriers. Distractions evaporate. Your inner critic is cut off and made silent. You're free to make progress without the anxieties and interruptions that can otherwise make creating something worthwhile difficult and even all but impossible.

Flow at School

Attending class can feel dull, especially if your instructor lacks charisma or presents the subject matter poorly. Your mind might wander, causing you to miss important material. As a result, facts and figures become harder to memorize. Assignments and projects become harder to complete. Exams become more difficult.

Being in flow will help you to pay attention in class. You'll be better able to learn and memorize the material presented, even if the lecture is tragically dull. Your notes will be more organized and complete. Regardless of the presenter's charisma, you'll feel more engaged by the subject matter.

This can give you an entirely different feeling when you attend class. It won't make a boring lecture or dull instructor more exciting. But it *can* help you to master the material so that completing assignments and projects and taking exams successfully is easier.

Flow during Sports

Many factors can negatively affect your performance in sports. This is so whether competing at an amateur or professional level. Your performance stems from more than physical ability or even mastery of the sport. You'll likely perform well if you're focused, relaxed, and aware of your body. Your performance will suffer if you're stressed, frustrated, or otherwise preoccupied.

Athletes report that when they're in the zone, their movements seem effortless to them. They say that calmness settles over them as stressors related to other areas of their lives fade away. They experience a greater sense of control and confidence. Self-doubt evaporates as they recognize that they're performing well.

When you compete in a flow state of mind, you can concentrate on the present moment rather than be worried about the outcome. You're fully absorbed in your immediate actions and circumstances. You're focused rather than distracted. You're engaged and enthusiastic rather than indifferent and apathetic.

The result? Not only will you perform at a higher level, but you'll likely find the experience more enjoyable, too.

Flow during Personal Leisure Time

We tend to think of our leisure time as trivial and frivolous. If whatever we're doing is unrelated to our jobs, families, or purposeful projects (e.g., painting the house, decluttering a room, etc.), it can't possibly be important, right?

Wrong. According to psychologists, the time we spend doing recreational activities is vital to our physical and mental health.[1] It helps us to manage stress and anxiety. It improves our mood. Depending on our activities, our leisure time can give us a sense of accomplishment, filling us with positive emotions.

Think about the activities you enjoy doing whenever you have free time. Here's a list of possibilities:

- Cooking
- Reading
- Playing guitar
- Gardening
- Fingerpainting
- Solving puzzles
- Knitting
- Playing chess
- Whittling

Have you ever done your favorite activities during your free time but couldn't fully enjoy yourself? Maybe you were troubled about other areas of your life. Perhaps you argued with your spouse about a trivial matter and felt regret. Maybe you were waiting for an important phone call and couldn't concentrate.

What if you could let go of every stressor looming over your head, if only temporarily? What if you could do your favorite recreational activities in a flow state?

You'd be able to immerse yourself fully. You could cook, read, or garden without internal distractions. You'd be able to truly *enjoy* your leisure time and reap the physical and mental health rewards accompanying it.

Flow Isn't Just about Productivity

The point I've tried to make in this section is that we can benefit from a flow experience in ways that may be unapparent and even counterintuitive. It isn't about increasing productivity and getting more things done (although this is a typical result of working in flow). Instead, it's about experiencing a more enjoyable, more rewarding life.

We feel more content when we routinely experience the level of engagement and immersion that a flow state makes possible. More satisfied with how we spend our time and attentional resources. Our thoughts become clearer, and our lives seem more meaningful to us.

This has a significant effect on our outlook. Rather than struggling to get through each day, we feel more connected to our actions as they relate to our goals and hobbies. We feel as if we're acting with more purpose and resolve. Consequently, each day feels less like a tedious struggle and more like a challenge over which we'll surely prevail.

Would you like to experience this feeling regularly? If so, let's lay the groundwork for learning to induce a flow experience.

---

1. Tonietto, G., Malkoc, S. A., Reczek, R. W., & Norton, M. I. (2021). Viewing leisure as wasteful undermines enjoyment. *Journal of Experimental Social Psychology*, 97, 104198. https://doi.org/10.1016/j.jesp.2021.104198

PART II

PREPARING TO ACHIEVE FLOW

∽

Fortunately, we don't have to wait for this state of mind to come over us. We don't need to rely on our muse. Once we understand the factors that trigger a flow experience, we can bring it about whenever it suits our schedule and circumstances.

There's nothing metaphysical or supernatural about it. It takes practice. As with any skill, the more you do it, the better you get at it and the easier it becomes.

Before we take the steps required to induce a flow state, we need to be aware of the factors that play a role. A little preparation goes a long way. It's akin to learning what a vehicle's steering wheel and pedals do before turning the key in the ignition.

To that end, this section will set the frame. We'll address the effects of fear on the flow experience and the elements that help to trigger it. We'll also explore the most common enemies of flow so you can avoid them before they present problems.

LAYING THE FOUNDATION

∼

You've undoubtedly experienced flow in the past. You may not have realized it then, but you were in the zone, completely immersed in what you were doing. You likely lost your sense of time. You may have failed to hear incoming calls and texts. Perhaps you even forgot a meal or two.

You weren't *trying* to get into a flow state. It simply happened. And you savored it because you were performing at full throttle and doing your best work.

The lesson is that when conditions are right, your mind can often find flow independently. This is the crux of being able to find flow at will. How effectively could you trigger a flow experience if you set those conditions in advance?

The Pivotal Role of Your Subconscious

Achieving flow requires you to feel at ease doing whatever you intend to do in the zone. This sense of calm arises from proficiency. If you've mastered a skill or activity, you'll likely feel comfortable doing it. This allows your subconscious to do a lot of the heavy lifting.

For example, let's suppose you're a competitive swimmer. You've been doing it for years, so much of it comes down to muscle memory. When competing, you don't have to think about how to perform each action of the freestyle, butterfly, or whatever event you're in. Your subconscious mind knows what it's doing and can do this for you. Because you don't have to think about each moment, you can get into the zone more quickly. Years of training have made this possible.

Now let's consider the opposite situation. You're learning how to swim. There's no muscle memory, so your subconscious can't take over. You're focused on how to perform each action and every stroke. You're concerned about breathing properly. You're concentrating on hitting the turn correctly. In this circumstance, it's nearly impossible to find flow. Your brain is working too hard because you don't feel at ease.

Your subconscious mind must be switched on before entering the zone. This can only happen if you're adept at the activity you're performing. Whether the activity is creative, physical, or intellectual doesn't matter. You must be practiced at it before your subconscious mind can be activated.

The good news is that this occurs naturally. The more experienced and skilled you are, the more eager and prepared your subconscious will be to jump into the gap.

How Your Routines and Habits Help You

Many people relish the idea of being spontaneous. Taking unplanned action in the spur of the moment seems fun and thrilling to them. But in reality, most of us thrive on routine. We're creatures of habit.

This is good news as it relates to learning how to trigger a flow experience. We noted above that our subconscious mind plays a critical role in achieving flow. We also pointed out that this part of our mind is activated when we do something we're skilled at. We can smooth the path toward entering a flow state by following routines that stimulate our subconscious.

We create a string of habits (a process called habit stacking) that we perform each time we desire to enter a flow state. These routines spring from patterns that we develop to prompt our subconscious mind. The routine triggers our subconscious mind, allowing it to handle the minutiae of our actions. This alleviates our conscious mind of this effort, allowing it to immerse itself fully.

The routines and habits you create for this purpose will be unique and based on your predilections. They might involve taking short walks outside, listening to specific types of music, or doing breathing exercises. We'll discuss this in more detail in *Part III*.

The Nonnegotiable Conditions of Flow

A flow experience requires that specific circumstances are in effect. Three conditions must be met before we can truly enter the zone.

First, we must have a particular objective in mind. Ideally, this would arise from something important to us (as opposed to pressure from our boss or others' expectations).

Second, we must be convinced that we can successfully perform the activity we're engaged in. We need to be confident that we can overcome any challenges we encounter.

Third, we must have a feedback loop in place. This feedback loop provides a continuing, on-the-spot assessment of our actions. It tells us whether we're on the right path toward achieving our objective.

When these three conditions are in place, triggering a flow state of mind is much easier. If they're not in place, achieving flow is practically impossible.

HOW FEAR IMPEDES FLOW

~

Fear can be good for us. It increases our situational awareness and protects us from danger. It encourages us to be cautious when bad decisions can lead to misfortune. In some situations, it can be imperative to our survival.

But fear can also be a stumbling block. Left unchecked, it causes us to feel stressed, anxious, and even panicked. This impairs our decision-making and can even paralyze our minds, making us incapable of action.

It isn't easy to focus when we're in this state. Unless we untangle this fear, enjoying a flow experience is nearly impossible. So let's take a closer look at this potentially detrimental emotion. We'll briefly discuss the types of fear you may encounter and how to manage them so they don't prevent you from achieving flow.

How Fear Hijacks Your Mind

Deep inside the brain resides two oval structures that together comprise the amygdala. Among other functions, the amygdala processes stimuli that it perceives as possible threats to our physical and emotional well-being. The amygdala prompts us to respond to negative stimuli in a manner that's likely to ensure our survival. When stimulated, it triggers a fight-or-flight response.

This is an oversimplification of a complex part of our brain. But it'll suffice for our purpose of exploring the flow experience.

In his book, *Emotional Intelligence*, psychologist Daniel Goleman coined the term amygdala hijack. This emotional response to potentially threatening stimuli overrides our brain's rational function. Reason and rationality are "hijacked" by the amygdala, which prompts us to react in ways that are disproportionate to our circumstances.

For example, suppose you're driving to work, and another driver unwittingly cuts you off. You swerve to the side in a moment of panic. You've safely avoided a collision, but you're enraged. You catch up to the offending driver, screaming and using your middle finger in ways that are unlikely to result in friendship.

Your amygdala has hijacked your brain, triggering a disproportionate emotional response. You're safe and unharmed but angry; this emotional state spurs you to lash out.

It's important to understand this process because the

stress and anxiety we experience at any given moment impede our flow. When we fail to manage our fears, we unconsciously allow them to obstruct our flow. Our stress levels rise, and our attentional resources are diverted to respond to the stimuli that caused it.

Athletes regularly experience this problem. Their anxiety and nervousness about an event (e.g., fear of failure) prevent them from focusing and getting into the zone. Their fear ultimately harms their performance.

Once we learn to manage our fears and control our emotional responses to negative stimuli, we become better equipped to trigger a flow experience.

10 Types of Fear That Block Flow

Before properly managing our fears, we must be aware of the ones that afflict us. These will vary from person to person. The fears that block your flow will differ from the ones that block someone else's. Here are ten common types of fear that hold us back.

1. Fear of failure
2. Fear of success
3. Fear of change
4. Fear of criticism
5. Fear of humiliation
6. Fear of missing out
7. Fear of making mistakes
8. Fear of the unknown

9. Fear of responsibility
10. Fear of commitment

You've almost certainly experienced many of the fears listed above. You may even be plagued by a few of them currently. You're not alone. Everyone suffers from them at some point, and some suffer from them regularly.

For example, I'm often beset by a fear of change and the unknown. According to my parents, this has been the case since childhood. I've learned to manage these fears in adulthood, but it took time and effort. The upside is that they no longer prevent me from entering the zone.

Likewise, achieving flow will be much easier once you manage the fears that routinely hold *you* back.

How to Overcome Fear and Anxiety

It's impossible to address this important topic here adequately. Entire books have been written on them.[1] Nevertheless, I can offer a few tips that have helped me manage my fears. You may find them helpful, too.

First, identify your fear. This advice may sound trite, but it's tempting to try to manage fear by avoiding or ignoring it. This doesn't work (I speak from experience). Before we can manage a particular fear or anxiety, we must be willing to face it. We must *own* it.

Second, record when you experience your fear and what circumstances trigger it. This may reveal behavioral patterns. Once they're exposed, it's easier to manage them effectively.

Third, when your fear rears its head, stop what you're doing and ask yourself whether it's rational. It's tempting to catastrophize. We often assume the worst will happen, even when our past experiences discredit such assumptions. This exercise helped me to realize that my fear of change is nearly always unwarranted.

Fourth, use your imagination to visualize succeeding despite your fear. For example, you have a job interview and are anxious about change. Close your eyes and imagine being hired and thoroughly enjoying your new job.

I don't want to trivialize the process of overcoming fear. It can be a complex and challenging ordeal, especially if deeply-rooted issues trigger the fears in question. Even so, the tips above have helped me, and I sincerely hope they'll help you, too.

---

1. *The Big Leap* by Gay Hendricks and *The Confidence Gap* by Russ Harris are excellent.

THE MANY TRIGGERS OF FLOW

∽

In the *Laying the Foundation* section, we talked about the three major preconditions of flow:

1. A straightforward objective
2. Confidence that you can overcome attendant challenges
3. A positive feedback loop

Each of these elements must be in place before achieving a flow state. Once we establish them, we've done half the work. From there, we can bring about a flow state of mind with the help of numerous reliable triggers.

Author Steven Kotler suggested 17 flow triggers in his 2014 book *The Rise of Superman*. He organized them into four distinct groups. Below, we'll explore these groups and discover how we can consistently employ their respective triggers to find flow.

4 Types of Triggers That Induce Flow

Flow triggers spur us to concentrate on the task at hand. They're sensory cues that drive us toward a flow state of mind. While entering flow at will is always intentional (we'll cover the steps in *Part III*), these triggers pave the way by functioning as behavioral prompts.

They can be categorized into four groups, defined by Kotler as follows:

- Cognitive triggers
- Environmental triggers
- Creative triggers
- Social triggers

Cognitive triggers occur in our minds. They include intense focus, having an explicit goal, possessing an appropriate skill level in relation to that goal, and having a means by which we receive feedback regarding our efforts. Because the latter three triggers are nearly indistinguishable from the three major flow preconditions, they're essential to diving into the zone.

Note: "appropriate skill level" doesn't simply mean we can execute the task. We must feel challenged by the task without feeling that it's impossible. We must feel neither bored nor distressed.

Environmental triggers occur in our surroundings. They include a risk of weighty consequences, a dynamic setting, and deep awareness of all external stimuli. Let's quickly unpack each of them. First, the danger of an undesired outcome impels our focus. For example, an athlete might dread losing a competition. This undesired outcome spurs their focus.

Second, a dynamic setting presents a level of randomness and uncertainty. It stimulates our senses and compels us to concentrate. For example, let's suppose you're white water rafting. The river's current and the positions of nearby rocks require you to focus.

Third, deep awareness of external stimuli refers to processing sensory data. An environment that offers a rich source of sensory stimuli encourages us to pay attention. We feel acutely connected to our surroundings, which frees up our attentional resources. For example, a hunter would be keenly aware of sounds, scents, and other sensory inputs.

Creative triggers share a complicated relationship with the flow experience. According to Kotler, they form a loop where one feeds the other. Creativity helps to trigger flow, which in turn stimulates further creativity. This process pulls us deeper and deeper into the zone.

According to Apple founder Steve Jobs, the creation of new ideas stems from recognizing connections among inputs. As he famously said:

> Creativity is just connecting things. When you ask creative people how they did something, they feel a little guilty because they didn't really do it, they just saw something. It seemed obvious to them after a while. That's because they were able to connect experiences they've had and synthesize new things."

This sentiment aligns with the use of creativity as a flow trigger. When we recognize patterns and connections, our brain releases the neurotransmitter dopamine. This sharpens our focus, helping us to enter a flow state.

Social triggers occur in group settings. We tend to think of the flow experience from an individual's perspective. But it can also be present amongst a group collaborating to achieve a shared goal.

Some of these social triggers are similar to those we've already addressed. These include intense focus, a clear objective, and a risk of an undesired outcome (e.g., failure). Other triggers noted by Kotler are exclusive to this category and are listed below using his phrasing:

- Good communication
- Familiarity
- Blending egos
- Sense of control
- Close listening
- Always say yes

A few of these triggers would benefit from clarification. *Familiarity* refers to a shared language among group members. It need not be spoken language (e.g., hand signals in baseball). It just needs to be understood by all members.

Blending egos means that no single member of a group receives the majority of attention. All members are involved and participate equally.

Sense of control refers to the freedom each member enjoys to address their responsibilities with the skills they possess. As the group pursues its shared goal, individual members are given latitude to perform their respective tasks in a manner that suits them.

Always say yes doesn't mean being a pushover or doormat. Instead, it means group members should build upon each others' contributions instead of disparaging or squabbling about them.

Those are the 17 flow triggers described and categorized into four groups by Kotler. Of course, being aware of them is only the first step toward employing them.

Which Flow Triggers Should You Focus On?

A few of the aforementioned flow triggers are non-negotiable. For example, achieving flow requires concentration, a crystal-clear objective, a feedback loop, and sufficient skills to achieve the goal while feeling challenged (i.e., cognitive triggers).

All are important and contribute significantly to

inducing a flow experience. But it's possible to find flow in their absence. For example, deep awareness of external stimuli may be unnecessary or less critical depending on our situation and the type of work we're doing. Likewise, Kotler's social triggers are less relevant if we work independently. Also, some triggers are arguably more open to personal tastes and circumstances.

I recommend experimenting with each flow trigger and monitoring how it affects you in light of your activity. For example, pursue activities that carry a risk of consequences and then note whether that risk sharpened your focus or distracted you.

Another example: perform your chosen activity in different environments (e.g., at home alone, in a bustling coffee shop, etc.). Then record how each one affected you. Did the stimuli in a dynamic setting stimulate your senses and help you to zero in on your work, or did they intrude upon your thoughts, making it difficult to concentrate?

The main point is that finding flow is a different experience for each of us. This book aims to help you to create a process that works for *you*.

THE MOST FORMIDABLE ENEMIES OF FLOW

∼

Flow triggers are pivotal to getting into the zone but represent only one side of the equation. The other side is just as important: flow blockers. These are the enemies of flow. Left unchecked, they'll prevent us from entering flow, even if we employ all the triggers available.

The good news is that we don't have to be victims of these flow killers. We can address them head-on to ensure they don't become barriers for us. Below, we'll examine the most oppressive flow blockers and discuss practical tips for resolving them. (Note: this is the most extended section in the book, but I promise it's a worthwhile read.)

Distractions

When distracted, getting into a flow state of mind is virtually impossible. Our attention is pulled away from whatever we try to accomplish, often in multiple directions.

We tend to think of distractions in the context of our physical surroundings. In the workplace, noisy coworkers, unimportant meetings, and idle gossip make concentrating difficult. Nearby construction workers, rowdy children, and neighbors who drop by unannounced can ruin our concentration at home. And, of course, we shouldn't leave out our phones, the internet, and social media.

Distractions can also occur internally. Our thoughts and emotions can derail our focus, preventing us from enjoying a flow experience. For example, we might worry about our finances, brood over our relationships, or agonize about recent decisions. Some of us also struggle with self-doubt (we'll address this particular nuisance in more detail below).

We can take steps to reduce and eliminate many distractions that frustrate our efforts to achieve flow. We can arrive early at the office before coworkers turn up. We can wear headphones to reduce noise and discourage interruptions. We can close our office door (for limited periods, at least) and say no to meetings that don't require our attendance.

At home, we can ask family members to refrain from interrupting us while we work (unless there's an emergency). We can set boundaries with neighbors, discouraging them from dropping by at their whim. We can create a task management system that allows us to temporarily disregard other duties, knowing they'll ultimately get done.

Our internal distractions are more complex. Many people find that regular exercise, sufficient sleep, and a healthy diet help them manage their thoughts and emotions. Others benefit from meditation, therapy, and visual cues and reminders. Our internal distractions are unique to each of us, and thus so too must be the steps we take to address them.

Multitasking

Many people take pride in their ability to multitask. They believe that they thrive in busy, even chaotic, circumstances, deftly able to divide their attention among multiple tasks. But this belief is mistaken and based on an illusion.

Our brains don't multitask in the way many presume. Rather than addressing multiple tasks simultaneously, our brain switches between them (aptly called "task switching"). The problem is that task switching imposes a steep price. We disrupt our focus and momentum whenever we shift our attention from one task to another. This is called a switching cost. Multitaskers impose this penalty on themselves whenever they attempt to address multiple tasks concurrently.

If we aspire to achieve flow at will, we must rein in our inner multitasker. Here are a few tips:

- Turn off your phone while you work (when doing so is possible).
- Maintain an *effective* to-do list (prioritize tasks and estimate how long it'll take to complete each one).
- Say no to others' requests and invitations if you lack the time (refer to your to-do list).
- Declutter your workspace.
- Write down errant thoughts to prevent them from consuming your attentional resources.
- Refrain from checking email while you work.
- Train yourself to single-task (start with small steps — e.g., single-task for five minutes in the beginning).

I took the above measures to break my multitasking habit. It took time, but it worked. If you're a chronic multitasker, I encourage you to try them.

Self-Doubt

Each of us struggles with an inner critic. This is an internal monologue that disparages our thoughts, decisions, and actions. It causes us to question our judgment, whittling our confidence and esteem. Left unmanaged, it can eventually open the door to feelings of shame, inadequacy, and other bleak emotions.

For some of us, this inner voice is our greatest adversary to entering a flow state of mind. We fixate on its criticisms, which amplifies our doubts despite its criticisms being groundless. We lose trust in our skills and knowledge, which handicaps our ability to achieve flow.

We must learn to silence our inner critic and eliminate our doubts regarding our competence and abilities. This is a prerequisite to finding flow. If your inner critic is out of control, try the following whenever it rears its head:

- Write down the charge made by your inner critic in the second person. For example, "I'll never find someone to love me" becomes "You'll never find someone to love you." This tactic severs your attachment to the claim. Rather than accepting it at face value, you're more likely to question it.
- Dispute the charge. Demand supporting evidence. Then, scrutinize the evidence. (It won't survive this challenge.)
- Recall incidents that counter the charge. For example, following feedback at your job, recall your successful projects.
- Imagine advising a friend whose inner critic has made a similar charge. For example, you wouldn't say, "You *are* incompetent and useless." Instead, you'd say, "You made a mistake. Big deal. Everyone makes mistakes. It's not the end of the world." Show yourself the same compassion.

The important thing to remember is that our inner critic's claims are baseless. They stem from gross exaggerations of past events. For example, following a breakup, it might suggest that we're revolting and will never find someone who loves us. Following constructive feedback at our job, it may insinuate that we're incompetent and useless.

This perspective is our inner critic's Achilles' heel. It betrays the falsity of its claims. Once we recognize its dishonesty, our critical inner voice's power over us diminishes and, with time, may even evaporate.

Perfectionism

Perfectionism is unrealistic. But many of us ignore this fact and pursue it nonetheless. Sometimes, this tendency is nothing more than a temporary desire. Reason eventually takes over, and we abandon the pursuit once we realize it's impractical.

But for some of us, perfectionism becomes an obsession. We're consumed by it and refuse to accept any outcome that falls short of this unreasonable, self-imposed expectation. When we fail to meet this expectation, we berate ourselves and feel unhappy, anxious, and discouraged.

Perfectionism shares a paradoxical relationship with flow. The more preoccupied we are with perfection, the less confident we are in our skills and abilities. Rather than seeing an activity as a challenge (an essential component of achieving flow), we see it as something that'll lead to failure. This outlook prevents us from achieving a flow state. We're so fearful of failing (i.e., being less than perfect) that we can't experience total mental absorption.

If you struggle with perfectionism, try the following tips. They'll help you to overcome it.

- When you make a mistake, remember that it doesn't mean disaster. Most mistakes are fixable. Some can be ignored entirely because they're inconsequential.
- Ask yourself whether the time, effort, and stress related to perfection are worthwhile in light of your goals. This encourages you to see the larger picture.
- Regard your efforts as a "first draft." First drafts contain mistakes. Acknowledge that these mistakes can be resolved later during subsequent drafts. This will help alleviate your fear of making them.
- Track and celebrate your progress. You can make a ton of mistakes and still accomplish something worth self-praise.
- Remind yourself why you're doing the activity. This encourages you to see the big picture rather than get hung up on the minor details.

Getting into the zone requires that we abandon our perfectionistic tendencies. We become genuinely comfortable with our abilities only after we cast aside our concerns about being perfect. The certainty that we can overcome whatever challenges we encounter replaces our anxiety. This confidence gives us the freedom to trust ourselves.

Stress

Stress is a stealthy flow killer. It grows in silence, feeding on our negative thoughts and emotions that spring from the challenging circumstances we experience. Once it establishes a foothold, it monopolizes our attentional resources. It neuters our ability to concentrate, taking over our headspace and raising our anxiety.

Sometimes, stressful circumstances are major traumatic events, such as a divorce, a severe injury, or the death of a loved one. More commonly, stress results from unresolved issues and more minor incidents. For example, we may feel stress due to money problems, a high-pressure workplace, isolation, and loneliness. We might experience stress because of an argument with our spouse, a conflict with a coworker, or a "fender bender" during our morning commute.

If we fail to manage our stress correctly, it'll accumulate until it controls our thoughts, decisions, and actions. This pervasive effect will foil any attempt to get into the zone.

If your stress level regularly reaches the point that you're unable to focus, try these tips for managing it:

- Make time for recreational activities. Pursue your interests. Read a novel. Listen to music. Play chess online. Make sure it's something you enjoy. Schedule this time on your daily calendar.
- Take care of your body. Exercise. Stretch. Walk.
- Take care of your mind. Meditate. Practice deep breathing. Avoid the news.
- Get plenty of sleep. Create an evening routine that improves your sleep (e.g., no electronic devices before bed).
- Spend time with people you can talk to honestly about your feelings and problems.

These suggestions are merely the tip of the iceberg. Comprehensive stress management requires a much deeper investigation. The tips above are an excellent place to start.

It's worth noting that the type of stress we're referring to here is *negative* stress. It raises our anxiety and triggers our fight-or-flight response. Eustress, a form of *positive* stress, is a different part of our brain chemistry. It excites, motivates, and energizes us. We might experience it while planning a vacation or starting a new job.

Overcommitment

It's easy to fall into the habit of saying yes to everything, even if we know we should say no. We want to help people and avoid conflict. We want to accept invitations. We don't want to miss opportunities or rewarding experiences. But this lack of boundaries makes it nearly impossible to enjoy a flow experience.

The problem is that when we say yes to everything, we overcommit. We inadvertently pack our calendars with so much stuff that we leave no time for ourselves. No time to relax and recharge. No time to pursue our interests. No time to manage our physical, mental, and emotional health.

Making matters worse, we worry about meeting others' expectations. If we agree to help someone, will that person be satisfied with the result? If we accept an invitation, will the person who extended it be glad they did so?

We end up feeling anxious and pulled in too many directions. Our state of mind becomes frazzled. The clarity and calm we need to achieve flow evaporate.

The simple solution is to learn to say no. But simple doesn't always mean easy. Indeed, you may need to unravel years of programming. Here are a few helpful tips for replacing your "yes" habit with a "no" habit:

- Always know what is important to you (this is where you should spend your time).
- Recognize that saying "no" rejects the request, not the person making it.
- Create a few graceful responses (e.g., "I'd like to help you, but I'm swamped right now.").

- Offer an alternative (e.g., "My schedule is packed today and tomorrow. Can I help you on Thursday?").
- Be candid and clear (say, "No, I won't be able to attend tonight" rather than "Umm, I'm not sure…").
- Grow comfortable with missing out.

Learning to say no is the best way to avoid the trap of over-commitment. It gives us the freedom to prioritize what's important to *us* rather than devoting our limited and precious resources to *others'* priorities. In the process, we avoid the fear and anxiety that result from being stretched in too many directions. Instead, we enjoy a sense of control and calm, which help clear the path toward a flow experience.

Burnout

Burnout occurs when we feel mentally and emotionally exhausted due to persistent stress. It's usually discussed in the context of our jobs. We work long hours under pressure, sometimes at jobs we dislike, and eventually, the constant deadlines, our lack of engagement, and poor work/life balance take an enormous toll. We end up feeling cynical and emotionally drained. We become anxious and irritable. Unchecked, burnout can lead to depression, self-isolation, and substance abuse.

This problem can also happen at home, an issue that's

becoming more prevalent as more people work remotely. A 2020 poll conducted by the employment website Monster found that 69% of telecommuters experienced burnout symptoms while working from home.[1]

Unsurprisingly, there's a negative correlation between burnout and flow. When we suffer the former, it's nearly impossible to experience the latter. While this reality is intuitive, research supports it. A review of 18 empirical studies published in 2022 found that common burnout symptoms (exhaustion, cynicism, disengagement, etc.) impede flow.[2]

Fortunately, if we're struggling with burnout, we can take action to manage and overcome it. Here are a few simple steps that can prove to be valuable in that regard:

- Connect with family, friends, and coworkers. Social interaction can alleviate stress. That said, avoid negative people.
- Rethink how you view the source of your burnout. For example, if you're a teacher, focus on helping your students instead of the frustration of working with administrators. If you're attending university, focus on the reasons instead of the workload. If you're a corporate employee, focus on your contribution to projects instead of the drudgery of your workday.
- Set boundaries. Say "no" more often.
- Take breaks regularly. Working nonstop is tempting, especially if you're working under

looming deadlines. But taking a few minutes to recharge can help keep stress at bay.
- Treat self-care seriously. Get sufficient sleep. Maintain a healthy diet. Exercise, even if only a few minutes each day.

Burnout is a serious matter, and not only because it prevents us from getting into flow. It can have a severe impact on our quality of life. When we take purposeful steps to manage or avoid burnout, we protect our mental, emotional, and even physical health. And this makes achieving flow at will much easier.

Lack of Clarity

Clarity is elusive. Clarity about our purpose. Clarity about our goals. Clarity about our priorities and intentions. When we know precisely what we're striving for, life feels simple. Our actions and decisions are deliberate and measured because they're motivated by an explicit objective. For example, a mountaineer aspires to reach the top of the peak they're climbing. This sense of clarity drives them and keeps them focused. It helps them to get into the zone.

We feel disoriented and aimless when we're unclear about our purpose, goals, and priorities. We begin to question our motives and second-guess our actions and decisions. Our lack of clarity makes it difficult to act and decide confidently. Flow is impossible in this state of mind.

Many things can wreak havoc with our sense of clarity. For example, conflict with a loved one, fixation on coworkers' expectations, and simple fatigue from lack of sleep can muddle our thoughts and erect a mental block.

So how can we gain a sense of clarity? How can we become clear about our purpose, goals, and priorities? The following tips will help.

- Write down specifically what you'd like to achieve in the short term. For example, *"I want a perfect score on my next exam,"* *"I want to beat my record in this sporting event,"* or *"I want to finish writing this novel by the end of the month."*
- Express why you'd like to achieve this goal. The plainer your reason, the greater your sense of clarity about the actions you need to take.
- Determine how you'll measure your success. Simpler is better. An example would be your score on your next exam. You'll know immediately whether you've achieved your goal.
- Deduce a worst-case scenario in the event you fail. This scenario will almost certainly be less severe than your imagination suggests.
- Create a contingency plan. Decide what you'll do if you fail to achieve your goal. Will you spend more time studying for your next exam? Will you modify your physical training regimen? Will you commit to writing more words per day?

We can remedy the ambiguity of our purpose, goals, and priorities by applying this procedure consistently and methodically. If we do so, we'll alleviate the anxiety that springs from taking action and making decisions in a state of aimlessness and uncertainty. Instead, we'll enjoy the calm, certitude, and even conviction that accompanies the pursuit of a clear, simple goal.

Once we can manage these issues, we can better trigger a flow experience. Managing them removes the most formidable roadblocks. At that point, achieving flow at will becomes a matter of following a simple action plan.

---

1. *Monster poll results from work in the time of coronavirus.* (n.d.). https://learnmore.monster.com/poll-results-from-work-in-the-time-of-coronavirus
2. Aust, F., Beneke, T., Peifer, C., & Wekenborg, M. K. (2022b). The Relationship between Flow Experience and Burnout Symptoms: A Systematic Review. *International Journal of Environmental Research and Public Health, 19*(7), 3865. https://doi.org/10.3390/ijerph19073865

PART III

10 STEPS TO ACHIEVING A FLOW STATE

∽

The flow experience varies from person to person. While some properties of flow, such as intense focus, effortlessness, and a feeling of control, are universal, others are not. They're unique and based on the activity as well as the individual.

For example, athletes often report that they become hyperaware of their heartbeat, their breathing, and the strain of their muscles while in the zone. Meanwhile, students claim that they commonly overlook meals and forget appointments and other commitments while they study in a flow state. Those who work at home report a sense of calm and contentment.

Although each of us experiences flow differently, the

process by which we can trigger it is remarkably similar. This is good news indeed. It means we don't have to rely on circumstances beyond our control aligning perfectly to enjoy a flow state. We can induce flow at will.

This section will teach you how. Fair warning: as with developing any skill, learning to trigger flow will take practice. I have included simple exercises that correspond to each of the ten steps to help in that regard. I strongly encourage you to do them, ideally at a pace that suits you.

Let's dive in.

STEP #1: DEVELOP AND FOLLOW A PRE-FLOW ROUTINE

∼

Most of us have daily routines that give our lives structure. Many are performed during the daytime, at our jobs or at home. We conduct personal rituals in the morning; they help us to kickstart the day with a positive outlook. We perform some in the evening; they help us to wind down and prepare for the following day.

These routines make us more efficient. They help us to get things done without forcing us to plan every action. For example, we don't have to think about brushing our teeth before bed. It's part of our evening ritual.

Routines play another critical role, especially useful for triggering a flow state of mind. They signal to our brains that something is about to occur. By doing so, they alert our brain and prepare it to focus on the forthcoming event.

For example, an athlete will perform a warmup routine before a competition. Their regimen lets their brain know that it should direct its focus and attention to their performance. Similarly, a student might conduct a pre-study ritual before opening their books. Their behavioral pattern during their ritual alerts their brain that it should focus its attentional resources on the upcoming study session. Other examples:

- An artist might doodle for ten minutes before immersing themselves in a piece.
- A chef might inspect their kitchen and review the evening's menu before preparing meals.
- A teacher might assemble materials and supplies for the day's instruction.

Steven Kotler[1] has noted that flow follows focus. We can use this same strategy to help induce a flow experience. By performing a pre-flow ritual, we can cue our brain to adopt a singleminded temperament. This ritual, once it becomes a habit, produces a near-Pavlovian effect. It urges our brains to concentrate on the task at hand.

Let's create a pre-flow routine. It's important to note that yours will be unique to you.

EXERCISE #1

First, write down activities that have helped you to focus in the past. Perhaps you've performed breathing exercises. Or maybe you've found that doing yoga is effective. Some people find that taking a walk does the trick. These are things you do *before* getting to work. Here are a few other activities to kickstart your memory:

- Doing certain types of puzzles (crossword puzzles, word searches, logic problems, sudoku, etc.)
- Listening to a specific type of music (e.g., melodic jazz)
- Using flashcards to perform memory exercises
- Reading long-form articles while taking notes
- Sitting still while focusing on a single thing (e.g., a podcast)

Second, write down environmental triggers that help you to focus. Some people find that working by themselves in a small room with no windows makes it easier for them to concentrate. Conversely, others find that working in a busy environment with background noise (e.g., a coffee shop or a bustling office) has this effect. Here are a few other triggers that people have found helpful:

- The sound of a ticking clock

- The ambient noise from a floor fan (I use this myself)
- A particular type of music (e.g., Mozart's piano sonatas)
- Low-volume chatter
- A minimalistic workspace
- Bright lighting
- Ample space (a feeling of roominess)

Third, create a pre-flow routine incorporating the things you've written down as the building blocks. Note that this may require experimentation. You may need to test several before discovering the one that best suits you. Take your time and have fun with this exercise.

Time required: 15 minutes

---

1. Aforementioned author of *The Rise of Superman.*

STEP #2: IDENTIFY YOUR PEAK ENERGY TIMES

∼

We know that focus precedes flow. But our ability to focus requires energy. When we feel lethargic, concentrating is difficult, especially for long periods. For this reason, we need to determine our peak energy times. This will help us to select times during the day (or evening) when we're best conditioned for a flow experience.

Our body possesses an internal clock. This clock governs three biological rhythms. You're likely familiar with the circadian rhythm. It's a 24-hour cycle regulated by daylight that affects our bodies in myriad ways. An example is the sleep-wake cycle. The absence of daylight cues us to go to sleep. The presence of daylight cues us to wake up.

A second type of biological rhythm is the infradian

rhythm. It lasts longer than 24 hours; depending on the rhythm, its interval can be measured in weeks, months, or much longer. Often cited examples include the menstrual cycle and pregnancy.

We're most interested in the third type of biological rhythm: the ultradian rhythm. Its cycle lasts less than 24 hours; depending on the rhythm, its interval can be measured in hours or even minutes and seconds. Examples include our heart rate, appetite, and the release of various hormones, such as cortisol.

The ultradian rhythm is the biological rhythm most closely associated with our productivity. It's the one that has the most significant impact on our energy levels throughout the day. Once we identify select ultradian rhythms, we can determine the optimal times to trigger a flow state.

One of the ultradian rhythms we need to examine is the basic rest-activity cycle (BRAC).

How Our Basic Rest-Activity Cycle Works

According to physiologist Nathaniel Kleitman, who proposed it in the 1950s, this cycle lasts approximately 90 minutes. During the first half, we feel alert and aware. It's easy to concentrate during this period. However, during the last 20 minutes of the cycle, we experience a period of weariness. Focus becomes more difficult.

Fluctuations in our energy level usually arise from the basic rest-activity cycle. Note that this cycle varies for each of us regarding when it occurs and its duration (it may last 80 minutes for you and 120 for someone else).

Another ultradian rhythm we need to investigate is the REM-NREM sleep cycle. This cycle lasts for approximately 90 minutes and has a lesser effect on when we experience peak energy times. But since sleep restores our energy reserves, it's crucial to understand how this cycle works.

A Brief Primer on Sleep

Each sleep cycle advances through four stages. The first three are known as **NREM** sleep, or non-rapid eye movement sleep, and are referred to as N1, N2, and N3. The final stage is called **REM** sleep.

During N1, our brain slows down, and our body attempts to release tension. This lasts up to seven minutes. During N2, our heart rate and breathing are slowed, and our muscles are relaxed. This stage lasts between 10 and 25 minutes. N3 is deep sleep. We're fully relaxed during this stage. It lasts between 20 and 40 minutes. If you've ever awoken feeling disoriented, you were likely in N3.

The brain becomes active during REM sleep, the last stage of the REM-NREM sleep cycle. This stage lasts between 10 and 60 minutes and is when we experience rich, detailed dreams. REM sleep is associated with memory and creativity. Experts also believe that it aids us in processing our emotions.

If we fail to get sufficient REM sleep, it becomes more

difficult for us to concentrate when we're awake. We feel tired and easily distracted. We become unable to think clearly. This makes it extremely difficult to experience flow over an extended period.

For us to determine our peak energy times, we need to do two things:

1. Identify our basic rest-activity cycle.
2. Learn how to accommodate our REM-NREM sleep cycle.

Below is a 2-part exercise designed to do precisely that.

EXERCISE #2

Part I: Monitor your basic rest-activity cycle

GRAB a pen and a piece of paper. We'll use them to track your body's cues during three successive work sessions. Try to do this exercise in a space with minimal distractions. Additionally, try to get a full night of *restful* sleep beforehand. Lastly, eat something so you're not distracted by hunger.

Let's assume a baseline BRAC of 90 minutes.

Write down the start time of your first work session. As

you work, pay attention to your alertness and ability to focus. Both will be high in the beginning. But they'll begin to wane at some point. We aim to learn how much time passes before they do so. Write down the time that you begin to find it difficult to concentrate.

Take a 30-minute break. The time you recorded is your new baseline. But we're going to validate it with two more work sessions.

Write down the start time of your second work session. Again, note your body and mind's cues. When you start to lose your focus, record the time.

Take another 30-minute break.

Let's run through this process for the final time. Write down when you start to work, and observe when your attentiveness begins to diminish. Record the time.

You should now have a reasonably good grasp of your basic rest-activity cycle.

Time required: 6 hours

Part II: Your REM-NREM sleep cycle

We're not going to monitor your sleep cycle. We'll assume it follows a natural 4-stage pattern: N1, N2, N3, and finally, REM sleep. Our goal here is to build habits that *support* that cycle. We'll do this by experimenting with practices that have helped others get better sleep and note whether these practices also help you.

Many things can interfere with our natural sleep cycle.

So the first step is to remove, or at least minimize these factors. For this exercise, refrain from the following before going to bed:

- Consuming caffeine (six hours before)
- Consuming alcohol (four hours before)
- Smoking tobacco (three hours before)
- Eating (three hours before)
- Drinking any beverage (three hours before)
- Using electronic devices (30 minutes before)

When you wake up, perform your regular morning routine. Give your brain a chance to acclimatize to being awake. Then record how you feel. Do you feel rested and alert? Or do you feel tired and groggy?

It's likely your sleep will improve. When you eliminate the most common factors that interfere with sleep, you allow your body to experience its natural **REM-NREM** sleep cycle through the night repeatedly.

Next, let's experiment with factors that aid in getting good sleep. For this part of the exercise, try the following:

- Make your bedroom quiet and dark.
- Maintain a comfortable temperature (consider room temperature and bed coverings).
- Go to bed at the same time each night.
- If you take afternoon naps, keep them under 30 minutes
- Exercise during the day.

- Create a bedtime routine (read, take a warm bath, listen to relaxing music, etc.).

As before, carry out your regular morning routine when you wake up. Afterward, note how you feel. Do you feel rested and alert or tired and groggy?

Many people struggle to enjoy quality sleep but neglect to take steps to improve it. This part of the exercise will help you to sleep better at night. That, in turn, will help you experience an undiminished basic rest-activity cycle during the day and ultimately identify your peak energy times.

Time required: 3 days

STEP #3: CREATE A DISTRACTION-FREE ENVIRONMENT

~

Flow is impossible when we're distracted. We can't fully immerse ourselves in an activity when our attention is diverted from it.

Once we're in a flow state, we can perform without interference. Our brain is so absorbed in what we do that distractions can't access and sap our attentional resources. We're immune to them.

But getting to that point is another matter. We need to create a distraction-free environment. So we need to be proactive toward minimizing distractions that would thwart our efforts to get into a flow state.

We discussed in *Part I* that distractions come in two forms: internal and external distractions. Here we'll focus on eliminating the latter. It may feel as though we're powerless to influence our immediate surroundings. But in reality, we can take simple steps to filter out most, if not all, environmental distractions. When we do so successfully, we reward ourselves with the mental clarity to trigger a flow experience.

7 Things You Can Do to Keep Distractions at Bay

Some of the external distractions we face are unique to our circumstances. For example, parents of young children experience interruptions unlikely to affect those without children (at least not to the same extent). Supervisors and managers encounter distractions that are unlikely to impact their subordinates.

Other external distractions are more ubiquitous. They affect most of us regardless of our circumstances. Examples include background conversations, meddlesome coworkers and family members, noisy construction, the internet, and our phones. Poor lighting, an uncomfortable chair, and a cluttered workspace can distract us.

It isn't easy to concentrate, much less enjoy a true flow experience, when these things constantly try to divert our attention. But we can filter most of them by doing a few simple things. If you continuously struggle with distractions, try these seven tips:

1. Activate your phone's "Do Not Disturb" feature.
2. Wear headphones (this will prevent drive-by chats and muffle nearby noise).

3. If you have a door, close it.
4. Close your email program.
5. Use an app to block your web access (Freedom is a good option that works on all platforms).
6. Work in an isolated space (e.g., conference room, home office, etc.) if possible.
7. Let others know in advance that you need to work undisturbed for a set period.

These seven steps will go a long way toward reducing most external distractions preventing flow. They might even eliminate some altogether.

Once we know the obstacles you face, we can work toward clearing them. Of course, your circumstances are unique to you. So let's do a quick exercise to identify the distractions that most threaten your attentional resources.

EXERCISE #3

IMAGINE DOING an activity that's important to you and that you do at home. Perhaps it's practicing the guitar. Maybe it's writing a novel. Or possibly it's learning a new language, studying for exams, or researching topics that are interesting to you.

Now, think about the things that typically distract you

at home. Write down all of them. Here's a list of common distractions at home to help you get started:

- Television
- Phone
- Family members
- Roommates
- Internet
- Household chores
- Noisy neighbors
- Visitors

Rate each one from 1 to 5 according to its impact on you (1 means "high impact" while 5 means "low impact"). For example, your phone may significantly threaten your focus, while your television might pose no threat at all.

Let's go through the same process for your workplace (assuming you don't work from home). Imagine working in your office or cubicle. What commonly distracts you? Again, write them down. Here's a list to get you started:

- Noisy coworkers
- Email
- Incoming phone calls
- Coworkers who drop by to chat
- Gossip
- Office politics
- Anxiety about pending deadlines

As you did for your home distractions, rate each one from 1 to 5. For example, you might discover that email is your biggest obstacle when trying to work, while workplace gossip never distracts you.

Too often, we work distracted without knowing precisely our stumbling blocks. This exercise aims to pinpoint the things that are most likely to prevent us from enjoying a flow experience. Here we identify them so that we can be more vigilant about avoiding them.

Time required: 15 minutes

STEP #4: DEFINE A CLEAR MISSION

∽

Having an uncomplicated, understandable objective is crucial to achieving flow. When we know what we're working towards, we act with a sense of purpose. Our objective drives our behaviors and decisions. It helps us to concentrate and prioritize. It compels us to act intentionally.

All of this may sound obvious. But consider how often we work, behave, and think without a clear mission. At our jobs, we operate under constant deadlines, pressure from our bosses, and the prying eyes of our coworkers. At home, we rush around doing chores and trying to keep up with a never-ending (and growing) list of to-do items.

We're definitely *busy*. We feel productive and purposeful. But we never experience a flow state of mind where time fades away, and we become completely absorbed by what we're doing. Instead, we end up feeling exhausted. Worse, despite our efforts, we often feel we're not making significant progress, like a mouse running on its wheel.

Before truly enjoying a flow experience, we must have a clear mission in mind. We need to identify the outcome we desire. What are we working toward? What do we hope to accomplish with our efforts? Once we have this clarity, we can more easily and reliably trigger a flow state.

How to Define a Crystal-Clear Mission

The first step is to recognize what motivates us. This may be easier said than done, particularly if we've never thought about it candidly.

Some people are motivated by fear. They take action to avoid unpleasant outcomes. Some are motivated by select incentives, such as a promotion, a raise, or the admiration of coworkers or loved ones. Some are inspired by accomplishing specific achievements. For example, a student may aspire to be the valedictorian of their class. A salesperson might aspire to break a company sales record.

Second, we need to consider the outcome we wish to bring about. What do we hope to achieve? Here it's helpful to refer to the five parts of a S.M.A.R.T. goal: **S**pecific, **M**easurable, **A**ttainable, **R**elevant, and **T**ime-Bound. Defining our mission in terms of these five attributes will give us the clarity, direction, and structure we need to act with purpose.

Doing these two steps will help us shed the ambiguity

that would otherwise make it difficult to focus. Our mind is less likely to wander. Distractions will have a lesser effect on us. Ultimately, defining our mission clears our path toward finding flow.

∼

EXERCISE #4

∼

THIS EXERCISE POSES a series of questions. Your answers will help to develop and refine a mission that meets the five criteria of a S.M.A.R.T. goal. This simple procedure will produce a crystal-clear mission.

First, what do you want to accomplish?

Be as precise as possible. For example, if you're studying for an exam, your answer might be, "I want to earn a perfect score." If you're competing in a sporting event, your answer might be, "I want to win first place." If you're writing a song on the piano, your answer might be, "I want to complete the first and second verses."

Second, how will you determine if you've achieved your objective?

We need numbers. That's the best way to measure progress and success. For example, if you aim to write a 90,000-word novel in three months, you might set your sights on writing 1,000 words each day. If you desire to learn a new language, you might aspire to master ten conversational phrases.

Third, do you possess the requisite skills or knowledge to accomplish your objective in the timeframe you've set?

For example, if you've just begun to learn to play the piano, don't aspire to play Beethoven's "Hammerklavier" by the end of the day. Even experienced pianists have difficulty playing that piece. If you're taking an algebra class, don't aspire to earn a perfect score on an advanced calculus exam.

Fourth, what does your objective mean to you?

Flow requires a clear mission and some form of intrinsic motivation (we'll explore this concept in detail in *Step #5*). For example, writing a novel might be important because it proves that you can do something most people consider remarkable. Earning a perfect score on a difficult exam might be important because it'll make your family proud of you. Learning a new language might be important because it'll allow you to communicate better with a particular friend or family member.

Fifth, what's your timeframe?

Setting a start and end time is helpful in two ways. It'll help you to monitor your progress and evaluate your success. It'll also help you to stay focused. Note that we're not talking about a timeframe for your flow experience. The passage of time matters less when you're in a flow state. Instead, we're assigning a deadline by which you want to achieve your objective.

The deadline keeps you on track with a sense of mild

urgency. For example, if you're writing a novel, you might aim to complete the first draft by the end of August. If you're learning to play classical piano, you might seek to fluently play Beethoven's "Sonatina in G major" by the end of the week.

Once you've established a clear mission, you'll find it much easier to trigger a flow state. Your mind won't be troubled by uncertainty. Instead, your attentional resources can be devoted entirely to the activity at hand.

Time required: 20 minutes

STEP #5: ESTABLISH YOUR INTRINSIC MOTIVATION

∼

We feel compelled to take action for myriad reasons. Some are beneficial to us, while others are detrimental. Some are healthy, while others are less so. And some aid us in triggering flow, while others can impede the process.

Sometimes, we take action out of necessity. For example, we maintain jobs to feed our families, clothe our children, and pay our bills. We work overtime to finish projects under strict deadlines.

Sometimes, we act in pursuit of external rewards. For example, we compete in sporting events for trophies; we help others to earn their gratitude; we start a side business to make an additional income.

Sometimes, we're compelled by *internal* factors. The rewards we enjoy arise from inside us. For example, we read a book because we find it relaxing; we volunteer because doing so gives us a sense of fulfillment; we exercise because we care about our health.

While all three sources of motivation can drive us to take action, only the last one will help us to slip into a flow state. We can experience flow only after identifying our intrinsic motivation for an activity. It's a prerequisite.

Intrinsic Motivation Explained

The best way to describe intrinsic motivation is to contrast it with *extrinsic* motivation. The latter follows a reward system. We're compelled to act by an anticipated result.

For example, we go to our jobs each day to earn money (or to avoid being fired). We complete a school project to earn a good grade. We help an acquaintance to receive their praise and gratitude.

Extrinsic motivation is neither bad nor wrong. It can be very effective in urging us to take purposeful action. This is especially true when we need to do tedious, difficult, or inconvenient things. But it won't help us to trigger a flow experience. For that, we need *intrinsic* motivation.

Intrinsic motivation springs from within us. We're compelled to act by our desire to do a particular thing. Rather than seeking external rewards (e.g., money, others' praise and gratitude, good grades, etc.), we do something because the act of doing it is rewarding in and of itself.

For example, we go to our jobs each day because we love what we do for a living. We help an acquaintance because doing so gives us a sense of fulfillment. We complete a school project because we're deeply interested in the subject.

When intrinsically motivated, we're more inclined to become engrossed with the task at hand.[1] Taking action becomes easier because we're doing something consistent with our interests. And because we're intensely focused and fully engaged, we're more capable of experiencing flow.

The 3 Pillars of Intrinsic Motivation

Research shows that intrinsic motivation requires three conditions: autonomy, competence, and relatedness.[2] These psychological needs must be met before we genuinely feel motivated to act.

Autonomy refers to our need to feel like we have a choice in what we do. We must feel we have options and control over which options we select. For example, we want to be able to choose whether to help an acquaintance rather than be forced to do so.

Competence regards our sense that we can bring about the outcome we desire. We must feel we possess the requisite skills and knowledge to achieve this outcome. For example, to feel intrinsically motivated to complete a school project, we must be confident that we know the subject well enough to do so successfully.

Relatedness refers to our connection to other people. We're social animals at heart, even introverts. We crave and thrive on social interaction and want to feel like we belong.

For example, we join a fitness class at a gym, feeling a sense of connection with other members. We play guitar with other guitar players (e.g., a "jam session") because we identify with their musicianship. We volunteer to help as part of a group effort knowing that the same goal drives other volunteers.

When these three psychological needs are met, we feel inspired and energized. We take action because doing so is inherently satisfying and rewarding to us. This intrinsic motivation, combined with elements from the other steps in this section, can help propel us into a flow state.[3]

EXERCISE #5

THIS EXERCISE WILL EXAMINE your motivations for doing one particular activity. We'll uncover whether these motivations facilitate a flow experience.

First, choose an activity. It can be something related to your job or something you enjoy doing in your leisure time. It's entirely up to you (napping doesn't count).

Second, ask yourself whether you perform this activity for external rewards or because it's inherently satisfying. Both may be the case.

Third, consider whether you have a choice in how you approach the activity. Do you enjoy a sense of autonomy?

Fourth, ask yourself whether you possess the necessary skills and knowledge to accomplish your goals. Do you feel competent while performing this activity?

Fifth, reflect on whether doing this activity connects you with others. It's unnecessary to work closely with others doing the same thing to feel a connection with them. Simply knowing that others find value in what you're doing is enough.

After you complete this short exercise, you'll know whether your motivations spring from within you. If they do, you're one step closer to being able to trigger a flow state at will.

Time required: 10 minutes

---

1. Bonaiuto, M., Mao, Y., Roberts, S. A., Psalti, A., Ariccio, S., Cancellieri, U. G., & Csikszentmihalyi, M. (2016). Optimal Experience and Personal Growth: Flow and the Consolidation of Place Identity. *Frontiers in Psychology*, 7. https://doi.org/10.3389/fpsyg.2016.01654
2. Ryan, R. M., & Deci, E. L. (2000). Self-determination theory and the facilitation of intrinsic motivation, social development, and well-being. *American Psychologist*, 55(1), 68–78. https://doi.org/10.1037/0003-066x.55.1.68
3. A growing volume of scientific research examining intrinsic motivation as a facet of neuroscience and flow has been published in recent years. One example (and a fascinating read):
   Di Domenico, S. I., & Ryan, R. M. (2017). The Emerging Neuroscience of Intrinsic Motivation: A New Frontier in Self-Determination Research. *Frontiers in Human Neuroscience*, 11. https://doi.org/10.3389/fnhum.2017.00145

STEP #6: COMMIT TO MONOTASKING

∼

Most of us multitask despite knowing that doing so is counterproductive.[1] We do it for several reasons, which change based on our circumstances.

Sometimes we feel bored. We're disinterested in tasks that we need to complete, so we distract ourselves by doing other activities at the same time.

Sometimes we're impatient. If something happens too slowly for our tastes, we fill the "downtime" by addressing other tasks (e.g., checking email while coworkers present ideas during meetings).

Sometimes we convince ourselves that we can get more done by multitasking. This is arguably one of the worst reasons to multitask because it's a delusion. (That is, unless you're among the two percent of the population that can do it effectively.[2])

We discussed multitasking in the chapter *The Most Formidable Enemies of Flow*. There we addressed the problem of switching costs. This is the high price we pay each time our brain shifts its attentional resources between tasks. We'll avoid retreading that ground here. Suffice it to say that multitasking, or task switching, interrupts our flow experience and can prevent us from triggering flow altogether.

So we need to commit ourselves to single-tasking, also known as monotasking. If we want to trigger (and maintain) flow, we must resist the urge to juggle multiple tasks and activities simultaneously. This is easier said than done, especially if we've become so accustomed to multitasking that we're practically addicted to it.[3]

How to Retrain Your Brain to Monotask

In the chapter *The Most Formidable Enemies of Flow*, I offered a few tips for reining in your inner multitasker. Some people will find those tips to be sufficient. If that's the case for you, feel free to skip this section and advance to Exercise #6 below.

Other people will need to retrain themselves to monotask. They need to unravel years of programming that compels them to multitask habitually. I recommend the following course of action for them and perhaps you.

First, incorporate time chunking into your day. Practice

single-tasking for short time chunks (e.g., five minutes). As your ability to focus improves, increase the duration of your time chunks. Ten minutes. Then, fifteen minutes. Then, twenty minutes. With practice, you'll eventually be able to break up your day into large time chunks, confident that you can monotask at will.

Second, schedule breaks as a formal part of your daily calendar. During breaks, avoid work and let your mind wander. This isn't the time to check your phone for texts. Nor is this the time to check your email. Instead, take a walk. Go outside and people-watch. If you work indoors, go outside and enjoy the fresh air. It'll clear your mind and prepare you for your next time chunk.

Time each break in proportion to the duration of the preceding time chunk. For example, take a five-minute break after a 20-minute time chunk. Take a 20-minute break after a 1-hour time chunk.

Third, develop the habit of completing tasks before moving on to others. If you can't finish a task by the end of your scheduled time chunk, return to it after your break. Complete it, then work on something else.

Admittedly, this may not always be possible. For example, you may need input from other people before you can complete a task. If you're forced to wait for this input, work on something else rather than allow that time to slip through your fingers. Assign a time chunk for the new task. Complete it even if you receive the input needed before the time chunk ends.

This 3-step protocol will help you to break the single-tasking habit. But note that it'll take time to retrain your brain. It might take weeks, or even months, depending on how ingrained your multitasking habit is. But the return on your time investment will make the process worthwhile. Not only will you be more productive, but you'll also be one step closer to gaining the ability to trigger flow at will.

∼

EXERCISE #6

∼

THIS EXERCISE IS simple and easy. You'll need your pen and a pad of paper.

First, create a heading titled "Distractions." Write down everything that might distract you during a scheduled time chunk. (Hint: you can expedite this portion of the exercise by referring to your notes from Exercise #3.)

Second, create a heading titled "Solo Tasks." Write down tasks and activities for which you need to focus and can complete without input from others. Here are a few ideas to get you started:

- Working on select reports related to your job
- Studying for exams
- Creating art (e.g., painting, sculpting, writing a book, etc.)
- Working out

- Training for a sporting event
- Learning a new language
- Building a website

Third, pick one of the items on your "Solo Tasks" list. Find a space where you can perform that activity. Then review your "Distractions" list and do everything you can to minimize or eliminate them (for example, turn off your phone).

Lastly, start a timer and work on the activity you selected for as long as you can without your thoughts being pulled elsewhere. The moment your thoughts drift, stop the timer. The amount of time that passed is your baseline. This is the time to beat as you retrain your brain to monotask.

Don't feel discouraged if your baseline is short. The goal is to improve, not to succeed right out of the gate. If you do this exercise regularly, you'll find that you can focus and monotask for progressively longer time chunks. And as your ability to do so grows, you'll find it easier to get into the zone whenever you desire.

Time required: 15 to 60 minutes

---

1. Uncapher, M. R., Thieu, M. K., & Wagner, A. J. (2016). Media multitasking and memory: Differences in working memory and long-term memory. *Psychonomic Bulletin & Review, 23*(2), 483–490. https://doi.org/10.3758/s13423-015-0907-3

2. Watson, J., & Strayer, D. L. (2010). Supertaskers: Profiles in extraordinary multitasking ability. *Psychonomic Bulletin & Review, 17*(4), 479–485. https://doi.org/10.3758/pbr.17.4.479
3. Neuroscientist Daniel Levitin noted the following in his book *The Organized Mind*: "multitasking creates a dopamine-addiction feedback loop, effectively rewarding the brain for losing focus and for constantly searching for external stimulation."

STEP #7: CHOOSE A CHALLENGING (BUT ACHIEVABLE) TASK

∼

Flow requires a balance between an activity's difficulty level and our skills or knowledge related to the activity. If the activity is too easy for us, we'll become bored. Our minds will wander, and it won't be easy to focus. On the other hand, if the activity is too challenging for us, we'll feel frustrated, discouraged, and overwhelmed.

For example, imagine that your job involves data entry. If you've performed this task for any length of time, you'll find it hard to engage fully. Your performance may even require little more than muscle memory. Your attention is likely to drift to other matters. Such a state does not support flow. It'll be difficult to induce it, and it'll be virtually impossible to maintain it.

Conversely, imagine that you're learning to play the piano. You're a beginner, yet decide to tackle Chopin's Étude Op. 10 No. 4, a notoriously difficult piece. You commit to learning to play it flawlessly by the end of the week. This task and your self-imposed deadline will be too challenging unless you're a prodigy. You'll end up feeling frustrated and discouraged. As with the data entry job, this state won't accommodate a flow experience.

So the activity must strike a balance if we wish to enter a flow state. It must not be too easy or too difficult. Given our expertise and understanding, it must present a challenge but still be achievable.

Here's a tip: we don't have to accept tasks as they are presented. We can adjust the challenge-ability ratio to support a flow experience better. If an activity fails to balance its difficulty level and our skillset appropriately, we can modify it to suit us.

How to Modify Activities to Strike the Right Balance

Let's start with too-easy activities. Too-easy activities can be made more complex, and too-difficult activities can be made easier. There's a simple method for doing each.

The simplest way to modify too-easy tasks and activities so that they're more challenging and less tedious is through gamification. Essentially, we turn the task at hand into a game. Or at least apply one or more elements of a game. This can take the form of points, time limits, or other rules.

For example, suppose your job involves data entry. You can gamify this task by trying to complete as many items as possible within a given time frame (e.g., 25 entries within seven minutes). If you can achieve this goal easily, move the goalposts (e.g., 30 entries within seven minutes or 25 entries within six minutes).

You can gamify nearly any task in this manner. Whether you're training as an athlete, practicing the piano, or studying for exams, applying game-playing elements makes tedious tasks more challenging and engaging.

Modifying activities that are too *difficult* requires a different approach. But it's just as simple as modifying activities that are too easy.

The simplest way to make too-difficult tasks and activities easier is to break them down into smaller constituent parts. Most complex tasks are composed of hard parts and easy parts. Once these are isolated, you can address the ones that match your mood and energy level.

For example, suppose you're writing a book that'll require a tremendous amount of research. Some sections of this book will be easier to write than others. Once you identify the parts that'll be difficult to write and the parts that'll be easier, you can decide which ones to work on based on your mood and energy level.

Note that you may need to gamify some of the easier sections of an activity if they're not challenging enough to keep you engaged.

EXERCISE #7

∼

This exercise has two parts. First, we'll modify a too-easy activity to make it more challenging and less tedious. Second, we'll modify a too-difficult one to make it easier and less frustrating.

Part I: Select one activity you'd like to perform in a state of flow but find too easy or monotonous to keep you engaged. It might involve studying, playing scales on the piano, or data entry for your job.

Now, write down three ways to gamify this activity. You could apply a point system, time limits, or fun rewards for reaching pre-determined milestones.

Try these three gamification methods the next time you perform the activity. Keep the ones that make it more engaging for you. Jettison the ones that don't.

Part II: Select one activity or project you'd like to perform in a flow state but find too difficult or complicated. It might involve a large science project for school, an elaborate presentation for your job, or creating a large-scale website in your free time.

Break down this activity into subtasks. For example, building a website may require researching, creating content, designing the navigation and layout, establishing its brand, and many other tasks. Write down a list that includes all of these subtasks.

Focus on doing one subtask when you're ready to tackle your project.

Time required: 20 minutes

STEP #8: MAKE SURE YOU'RE RESTED, RELAXED, AND ALERT

∽

It's difficult to experience a flow state when we feel exhausted or anxious (or worse, both simultaneously). We lose our focus and become more susceptible to distractions. Our patience wears thin, and we become irritable and easily frustrated. We can't enjoy ourselves, even when doing something that usually makes us feel content.

We need rest.

When we think of rest, we usually think of sleep. But they're not the same thing. Sleep is merely one facet. Of course, good-quality sleep is essential to feeling rested. But many people routinely enjoy sound sleep and still feel worn out and high-strung each day. There are more pieces to this puzzle.

It turns out that there are several types of rest we need

to perform at a high level. We must experience all of them regularly. Doing so will remove obstacles that might otherwise hamper, disrupt, or abbreviate our flow experience.

Seven Types of Rest We Need

Life can be exhausting. We often feel thoroughly depleted — if not physically, then emotionally. We rush each day to get things done, fulfill our responsibilities, and remain available and present for the people we care about.

This is the road to chronic fatigue and burnout. As you can imagine, it is not conducive to flow. Fortunately, we can avoid this problem by getting the proper rest in the following areas.

Physical rest — this includes sleep (naps count). But it can also include stretching, massage, and deep breathing. Any activity, active or passive that relaxes our body is beneficial.

Mental rest — feeling physically rested but mentally exhausted is possible. It's common, even. Our focus dwindles, our memory falters, and we become irritable. We need to give our brains a break regularly. Taking short walks, doodling, journaling, or meditating... all can be useful.

Emotional rest — all of us have emotional needs. If these needs are unmet, we begin feeling isolated, frustrated, and overwhelmed. We can avoid this outcome by expressing our thoughts (i.e., refusing to hide them) and saying no more often to people.

Creative rest — we use creative thinking more often than we imagine. We use it to solve problems, plan events, weigh risks, make decisions, and communicate. To avoid a deficit in this area, we should look for opportunities to appreciate things outside our regular routine (e.g., nature, the arts, etc.).

Sensory rest — our senses are pummeled each day continuously. Sensory overload has become the norm thanks to our phones, computers, and the constant background noise in our surroundings. We need to "unplug" periodically to avoid overstimulation. This can include doing a digital detox[1] to simply closing our eyes for a few moments.

Social rest — some relationships are exhausting while others are invigorating. The former can quickly overtax our emotions (and patience). The latter rejuvenates and exhilarates us. We can avoid feeling drained socially by spending more time with people whose company we genuinely enjoy.

Spiritual rest — this stems from our belief system, creed, and even worldview. It may include religion and worship, a particular philosophy on life, or a connection to others in pursuit of something larger than ourselves. Feeling rested can give us purpose and inspiration. A deficit can lead to depression and despair.

As you can see, rest comes in many forms. Most people overlook one or more of them and never feel truly rested, relaxed, and alert. It's no coincidence that they rarely, if ever, experience a flow state of mind.

EXERCISE #8

IN THIS EXERCISE, we'll brainstorm simple ways to improve how you feel in each of the seven areas described above.

Grab a pen and a piece of paper. Create seven headings, one for each type of rest. Leave enough space beneath each heading to write a few sentences.

Now, one by one, come up with activities you can do to help you feel rested in that area. Write them down.

For example, under the heading "Physical rest," you might write the following:

- Take a 25-minute nap at 12:30 p.m. each day.
- Go to bed at 9:30 p.m.
- Get up and stretch every 90 minutes.

Under the heading "Sensory rest," you might write:

- Turn off my phone between 6:00 p.m. and 8:00 p.m.
- Avoid social media until after lunch.
- Use noise-canceling headphones at work.

Under the heading "Social rest," you might write:

- Stop hanging out with Barry on the weekends.
- Say no whenever Barbara asks me to do her work.
- Ask John if he wants to join me for breakfast each Monday morning.

The purpose of this exercise is twofold. First, it draws our attention to facets of "rest" that we may overlook. Second, it allows us to think up ways to feel more rested in each area. The more rested we feel across all seven areas, the less stressed and frustrated we'll feel, and the easier we'll be able to trigger a flow state.

Time required: 25 minutes

---

1. A digital detox is the practice of intentionally refraining from using phones and other technology for a period of time.

STEP #9: USE THE FLOWTIME TECHNIQUE

One of the most common obstacles to getting things done is procrastination. Once we *start* doing something, it's easy to *continue* doing it. The tricky part is getting started.

Many people use the Pomodoro technique to counter their tendency to procrastinate. Developed by Francesco Cirillo, it encourages short work sessions followed by short breaks. Specifically, a 25-minute work session is followed by a 5-minute break. This comprises one pomodoro. Four pomodoros are followed by a 15-minute break.

This is an effective technique for combating procrastination. It makes getting started easy. Additionally, it aids concentration and helps to repel distractions.

Many people use the Pomodoro technique to trigger a flow state. The idea is that flow is impossible if they can't get started. But this technique is unsuitable for this purpose.

Recall that during a flow state, our sense of time erodes. It passes without our notice. For this reason, the rigidity of the Pomodoro technique is incompatible with a flow experience. A timer that sounds off after 25 minutes will likely *interrupt* our flow rather than encourage it. Imagine being completely absorbed in what you're doing when your timer goes off and disrupts your concentration. Taking a 5-minute break at that point may be counterproductive. The timer and pomodoro become a hindrance rather than a help.

We need a different method. We need an approach that encourages focus, immersion, and engagement without restricting us to arbitrary time limits.

The solution is the Flowtime Technique.

The Flowtime Technique Explained

This approach rectifies the inflexible nature of pomodoros. Rather than prescribe arbitrary time limits on our work sessions and breaks, it allows us to work in accordance with our focus and momentum. This makes it easier to trigger and maintain a flow experience.

The Flowtime Technique urges us to choose a single task or activity to work on. We note the time that we start and then work as long as we can in a focused manner. We stop working when our focus wanes, and we need to take a break. We note the time we stop and the work session's duration.

Then, we take a break until we feel ready to start a new work session. At the end of our break, we record its duration.

This strategy gives us the latitude to work in line with our focus and momentum and allows us to track both for any activity. Patterns will appear over time. The more we do it, the stronger the patterns will become.

You can practice the Flowtime Technique by recording everything on paper or digitally. Make the following columns:

- Activity
- Start time
- End time
- Duration
- Break

When you start a task or activity, write down what you're working on and the time of day. When you stop working, record the time of day again. Calculate the length of your work session before you take a break. After you've finished your break, record how long it was. Then, repeat.

I prefer to use old-fashioned tools, such as pen and paper. But again, that's entirely up to you. Here's how your notes might appear on a spreadsheet after a full day:

	Activity	Start Time	End Time	Duration	Break
2	Practice scales on piano	7:00 a.m.	7:40 a.m.	40 minutes	15 minutes
3	Work on client project	7:55 a.m.	9:20 a.m.	1 hour, 25 minutes	40 minutes
4	Study for licensing exam	10:00 a.m.	11:15 a.m.	1 hour, 15 minutes	20 minutes
5	Respond to texts & emails	11:35 a.m	11:50 a.m.	15 minutes	40 minutes (lunch!)
6	Compose recital song	12:30 p.m.	2:35 p.m.	2 hours, 5 minutes	30 minutes
7	Write short story	3:05 p.m.	4:55 p.m.	1 hour, 50 minutes	35 minutes
8	Review & prep	5:30 p.m.	5:55 p.m.	25 minutes	Quitting time!

Flowtime Technique example

One quick note: many people who practice the Flowtime Technique include a column for interruptions in their notes. They record how many interruptions they endured during each work session.

I find this practice to be of limited use because knowing the number of interruptions provides little insight regarding how to avoid them. For this reason, I prefer to keep a separate "interruption log." When I am interrupted, I record when the interruption happened, the type of interruption (e.g., phone call, unannounced visitor, etc.), how long it lasted, and any follow-up action I need to take. These details provide more insight and are thus more actionable.

You may have noticed that the Flowtime Technique is similar to time chunking. They are indeed close cousins and offer the same degree of accommodation.

It's time for an exercise.

∼

EXERCISE #9

In this exercise, we'll practice using the Flowtime Technique.

First, create a matrix or table on paper or in your favorite spreadsheet program. It should mirror the columns in the image above.

Second, choose a task or activity you want to work on. It can be related to your job, hobbies, or even something you do during your leisure time (e.g., reading a novel). Describe it briefly in the first column of your matrix.

Third, record the time of day that you start working on this activity. Continue working on it until you start to lose focus and your thoughts begin to drift. Stop working and record the time of day.

Fourth, take a short break. The length of your break is entirely up to you. The important thing is to be aware of when you're ready to start a new work session. When you're ready to end your break, record how long it was.

Do this for an entire day. If you've never used time chunks or practiced the Flowtime Technique, I recommend doing this each day for at least a week. Then, review your notes and look for patterns:

- How long were you able to focus and feel wholly immersed in a particular activity before needing a break?
- How long did you need a break before feeling refreshed and ready to start a new work session?

- What differences in these regards do you observe between distinct tasks and activities? (Some will be more demanding than others.)

Once you've repeated the Flowtime Technique for a week or longer, you'll have a firmer grasp on how your mind prepares for, performs, and recovers from various activities. This will give you valuable insight into your ability to trigger and maintain flow.

Time required: 24 hours (minimum)

STEP #10: CREATE A FEEDBACK LOOP

> I think it's very important to have a feedback loop, where you're constantly thinking about what you've done and how you could be doing it better."
>
> — ELON MUSK, FOUNDER OF TESLA, SPACEX, AND OPENAI

Being in a flow state involves more than focus, immersion, and engagement in the task at hand. It requires that we can determine whether we're performing effectively. We need to know *how* we're doing in addition to *what* we're doing.

In the chapter *Laying the Foundation* (ref. to Part II), we broached the need for a positive feedback loop. We must have a way to monitor one or more aspects of our performance while we're in a flow state. This feedback gives us an opportunity to adjust our actions in the event they're ineffective or unsuccessful. The upside is that we enjoy a growing sense of achievement as we make continual progress toward our goal.

Feedback Silences Our Inner Critic

A positive feedback loop also encourages us to focus on moving forward rather than fixating on our mistakes. It dampens our inner critic's voice, allowing us to allocate our attentional resources more productively. We become less inclined to overthink or second-guess our actions and less susceptible to the attendant stress and frustration. Instead, we can rationally gauge our performance and make informed adjustments as necessary.

For example, imagine that you're training to run a marathon. If this is your first marathon, you'll need to train for several weeks, increasing your mileage each week. You can create a feedback loop by establishing weekly milestones based on distance and pace. You can thus monitor your progress and adjust your training as needed.

This mutes your inner critic. Rather than feeling distressed about being able to complete the marathon, you can focus on meeting your milestones. If you meet them successfully, you'll feel accomplished as you advance through your training. If you fail to meet them, you can adjust your training regimen.

Either way, you'll feel more relaxed and confident that you're on the right track. This self-assurance will silence your inner critic and free you to become fully immersed in your training.

EXERCISE #10

THIS EXERCISE IS SIMPLE, easy, and takes minimal time. But don't underestimate its usefulness. If you do it regularly, you'll find it's much easier to get into — and maintain — a flow state of mind.

First, choose an activity. Studying, working out, cooking, gardening, writing a novel, building a website, creating a presentation for your job… any activity will suffice.

Second, think about what will make you feel accomplished as you perform this activity. For example, studying for an important exam might involve the number of pages you read from your textbook. If you're writing a novel, it may entail the number of chapters you complete. If you're building a website, it might concern the sections you design. Write down your thoughts.

Third, create small milestones based on your notes from the previous step. For example, let's suppose you're writing a novel. You might set pace-based and word-based milestones, such as "write 250 words in 30 minutes."

Lastly, perform the activity. As you do so, monitor your progress. Are you on track? If so, great. If not, make adjustments. For example, you might discover that writing 250 words in 30 minutes is unrealistic. This is valuable feedback. Adjust your milestone to "write *200* words in 30 minutes." Continue to write and note your progress.

This practice will silence your inner critic and help you work without its useless (and fallacious) criticisms. You'll be able to respond positively and purposefully to the feedback you receive rather than overreact to fabricated failures.

Time required: 15 minutes (for steps 1 through 3)

SOLVING THE FLOW PUZZLE: A 60-SECOND RECAP

～

As I was wrapping up *Part III*, I realized that you might find useful a quick recap of the concepts we've covered. While I want to avoid rehashing our conversation, I also recognize that we've covered a lot of actionable material. Summing up the key points will be beneficial.

So, we're going to do exactly that in under 60 seconds. Start the clock.

Use Routines: The Unsung Hero of Flow

Routines do more than give our lives structure and make us more efficient. They signal to our brains that something is about to happen. Routines prepare us and put us in the right frame of mind — in this case, to enter flow.

Accommodate Your Natural Rhythm

Our energy levels ebb and flow throughout the day according to our basic rest-activity cycle (BRAC). Once we determine our BRAC, we can schedule flow sessions around our peak energy times.

Go on an Attention Diet

Flow requires deep focus. The problem is that countless distractions seek to ruin our focus every day. When we avoid distractions (e.g., phone, chatty coworkers, social media, etc.), we keep our focus fit and trim.

Act with Purpose

We need a clear goal that informs our actions and pushes us forward. This goal doesn't need to be awe-inspiring; it just needs to be precise.

Look Inward for Inspiration

It's easier to trigger flow when we act with purpose. The best place to find this purpose is within us. When motivated by our interests (rather than external rewards), we're more likely to feel engaged and experience total immersion.

Abandon Multitasking Mode

Multitasking is anathema to flow. It imposes severe switching costs and erodes our attentional resources. When we single-task, staying focused and in the zone is easier.

Optimize the Challenge/Skills Ratio

The task at hand should be neither too easy nor too hard. It should pose a challenge but be achievable. Entering flow is easier when we find the right balance.

Take Advantage of All Types of Rest

Sleep is essential, of course. But feeling *truly* rested, physically, mentally, and emotionally, requires more than sleep. When we get all types of rest, we're more capable of triggering and maintaining flow.

Get To Know Pomodoro's Easygoing Cousin

The Flowtime Technique is superior to pomodoros for getting in the zone. It gives us more freedom to work and concentrate in line with our circumstances (e.g., energy level, schedule, etc.).

Evaluate, Adjust, and Move Forward

We need a way to monitor our performance. That's the only way to know whether we're on the right track. A feedback loop keeps us informed and helps us to make adjustments based on our progress and objective.

We Are Not Done

We now have the building blocks we need to trigger a flow experience. Keep in mind that getting in the zone *at will* takes practice. But we know what's involved and can develop the skill at a pace that suits us.

We're not done. There's more material to cover. In *Part IV*, we'll explore select aspects of flow to gain a better understanding and greater awareness of it. That'll help us to enjoy maximum benefit from it.

PART IV

GREATER AWARENESS ABOUT YOUR FLOW STATE

∽

Knowing how to enter a flow state is the most crucial part of the puzzle. But there are other pieces to consider. When we familiarize ourselves with them, we gain a greater appreciation for how flow works and how to make the most of it.

This section will cover several critical details about flow that extend beyond its inducement. We'll learn to recognize when we're having a flow experience so that we can embrace it deliberately and confidently. We'll discuss the range of flow and how we can capitalize on flow variants. We'll explore how to stay in a flow state once we've entered it. And lastly, we'll investigate the "dark side" of flow (there are indeed risks).

7 SIGNS YOU HAVE ACHIEVED A FLOW STATE

∼

Flow is a subjective experience. It's unique to the individual. Your experience will be different from everyone else's. Having said that, several features are practically universal. You'll observe them whenever you're in a flow state.

There are many tools used today to evaluate and measure flow. These include the Dispositional Flow Scale,[1] the Situation-Specific Flow Questionnaire,[2] and the Activity Flow State Scale (AFSS).[3] While these tools have proven effective in controlled research and observational studies, they require substantial time and effort. Using them to determine whether we've achieved flow in our daily activities is, in my opinion, a poor investment.

There's a more straightforward method. In the spirit of the 80/20 principle, we can use this method to make an imperfect but reasonably accurate assessment. We just need to know what to look for.

If we're ever uncertain whether we've achieved flow, we should look for the seven signs described below. We experience each of them sporadically throughout our lives. But if all seven are present at once, it's almost certain that we're in the zone.

Sign #1: Our actions require minimal thought

When we perform a task for which we lack the requisite skills or knowledge, we think cautiously about what we're doing. We try to avoid mishandling the task, failing, and reaping the derision or pity of others. We plan and execute with care.

Conversely, when we're in the zone, taking action feels effortless. The task at hand still requires our attentional resources. But we're so focused, aware, and confident in our abilities that there's minimal anxiety.

For example, recall how you felt while learning to drive. It was likely a nerve-wracking experience. You had to think about every action (e.g., crank the motor, shift into reverse, scan the mirrors, etc.). A single mistake could have been disastrous.

Driving is a different experience for you today. Years spent behind the wheel have made you proficient and given you confidence. Driving requires your attention, but you no longer have to think about everything you do. It has become second nature to you.

It feels intuitive.

Sign #2: We feel in total control

Experience, proficiency, and confidence produce another effect: we feel in control in the moment. We know what we're doing, know what we want to accomplish, and can imagine the end result. We feel that nothing will be left to fate. Every factor that might influence the outcome is in our control.

For example, imagine that you're a skilled chef. You're preparing a dish that you've prepared hundreds of times. You know every ingredient. You know precisely how long select items should cook and rest. You can envision the plate presentation. You feel in total control of the outcome.

This sense of total control is technically illusory. External factors, such as an emergency, can potentially disrupt you. But this fact is immaterial. Simply *feeling* in control because of your experience, proficiency, and confidence is a sign of being in flow.

Sign #3: We experience joy while doing the activity

We discussed the importance of an internally rewarding activity in *Step 5: Establish Your Intrinsic Motivation*. We find such activities interesting, exciting, and satisfying. We do them because we *enjoy* doing them rather than feeling pressured by external factors.

For example, think about your favorite hobby. Maybe it

involves cooking, reading, or playing a particular sport with friends. Perhaps you enjoy photography, solving jigsaw puzzles, or playing the guitar. Whatever the activity, you probably experience a deep sense of contentment whenever you do it. You feel relaxed, confident, and engaged. You may even find that the world around you fades away as you become completely engrossed in this activity.

When this occurs, you're likely close to — or already in — a flow state.

Sign #4: Our awareness narrows

We experience broad-scale awareness during most of our waking hours. Our attention branches off in many directions based on internal and external stimuli.

For example, we hear coworkers chatting and wonder what they're talking about. We note heavy clouds in the sky and fret about a rainy commute home. We smell savory food and realize that we're hungry.

In contrast, our awareness tightens when we're wholly engaged in what we're doing. Our cognitive field of view narrows so that we become hyperaware of the activity in front of us and much less aware of what's happening around us. In this state, we're far less likely to be distracted by internal and external stimuli.

For example, we may not hear coworkers chatting despite them being nearby. We might forget to eat lunch or dinner even if we haven't eaten for hours. We may be utterly oblivious to the weather despite sitting next to a window and looking outside.

All of our attentional resources are devoted to the task at hand.

Sign #5: We act with zero self-consciousness

Self-consciousness can have a beneficial effect on our behaviors and decisions. For example, we might feel self-conscious when we make mistakes that impact others. A healthy effect would be the impulse to take responsibility for our mistakes and make atonement (if appropriate).

Most times, however, self-consciousness has a harmful effect on us, particularly when we fail to manage it. It overtakes our headspace, causing us stress and anxiety as we try to fit in, avoid embarrassment, and meet others' expectations. It can become debilitating for some people.

When we're wholly focused and engaged, self-consciousness doesn't affect us. We act without worry regarding our mistakes, other people's expectations, and how others perceive us. Our inner critic no longer stifles our behaviors and decisions. Our fears melt away, and we experience a feeling of peace and confidence.

Sign #6: Time awareness evaporates

You can relate to watching the clock if you've ever held a boring job. Seconds ticked by at a snail's pace, and it may have seemed as though lunchtime (or quitting time) would never arrive.

Conversely, if you've ever worked under a strict and looming deadline, you probably watched the clock and experienced a different feeling. Perhaps you felt stressed and under intense pressure and wondered whether you'd finish in time.

In both cases, you possessed acute time awareness. Had someone asked you the time, you'd likely have been able to tell them without checking.

This time awareness dissolves when you're entirely preoccupied with what you're doing. You're aware of the present moment and mindful of everything you do in that moment but heedless of time's passage.

You're likely in the zone.

Sign #7: Total clarity about what we're doing

Much of what we do each day is done without complete comprehension. We may understand what we're doing in the moment but lack insight regarding *why*.

For example, we expertly prepare a report for our boss without knowing who will ultimately use it and for what purpose. We participate in a league sport but do so more out of habit than genuine interest in the sport or our teammates. We enroll in training courses or college classes without a concrete plan for using the instruction.

Compare this to the times when we act with absolute clarity regarding what we're doing and *why* we're doing it.

We have a clear goal in mind. We know what we want to accomplish. And we possess the skills and knowledge to bring about that outcome. There's no ambiguity.

This state of mind is an onramp to a flow experience.

All Signs Point to Flow

This doesn't necessarily mean we're in a flow state. We undoubtedly experience one or more of the above signs in practice during a typical day. But when we experience all seven simultaneously, we're either on the cusp of flow or already enveloped in its grasp.

---

1. Riva, E., Riva, G., Talò, C., Boffi, M., Rainisio, N., Pola, L., Diana, B., Villani, D., Argenton, L., & Inghilleri, P. (2017). Measuring Dispositional Flow: Validity and reliability of the Dispositional Flow State Scale 2, Italian version. *PLOS ONE, 12*(9), e0182201. https://doi.org/10.1371/journal.pone.0182201
2. Magyaródi, T., Nagy, H., Soltész, P., Mózes, T., & Oláh, A. (2014). Psychometric properties of a newly established flow state questionnaire. *The Journal of Happiness and Well-Being, 1*(2), 89–100.
3. Payne, B. R., Jackson, J. J., Noh, S. R., & Stine-Morrow, E. a. L. (2011). In the zone: Flow state and cognition in older adults. *Psychology and Aging, 26*(3), 738–743. https://doi.org/10.1037/a0022359

MICROFLOW VS. MACRO FLOW

∽

Until now, we've discussed flow with the assumption that it's a binary circumstance. We're either *in* flow or *not* in flow. But this is an inaccurate impression. Myriad levels of flow fall across a vast range. This powerful state of consciousness is nuanced.

When we acknowledge the fluid and variable nature of flow, triggering it becomes less daunting. We no longer have to worry about creating the "perfect" environment to enter a flow state. We no longer need to concern ourselves with meeting every precondition of flow. We can enjoy the flow experience even if it's a more modest form than we desire.

What Is Microflow?

In *Part III: 10 Steps to Achieving a Flow State*, we addressed the requirements of a full-scale flow experience. We noted the importance of having a clear mission; we talked about why we should cater to our peak energy times; we discussed the value of intrinsic motivation and the need for a feedback loop.

But what if these and all other preconditions are not in place? Does this mean a flow experience is impossible?

Simply put, no. We can still avail ourselves of a flow state of mind. We can take advantage of "microflow."

Microflow occurs when some of the preconditions of flow are met but not all. Circumstances are imperfect for getting in the zone.

For example, suppose you're working on a project related to your job. You've eliminated distractions from your immediate environment, identified a feedback loop to evaluate your progress, and found the task challenging yet achievable. Unfortunately, you're not working during your peak-energy time. Nor are you clear about your mission.

In this situation, all is not lost. You can still enjoy a lighter form of flow. Your level of immersion may be reduced. Your level of concentration and engagement might be diminished. And the duration of your flow experience may be abbreviated. But you can still reap its many benefits (e.g., greater creativity, less resistance from your inner critic, increased productivity, a sense of joy and satisfaction, etc.).

In this case, you're experiencing microflow. It's arguably an inferior experience compared to a full-blown flow state. But it can still be remarkably productive and highly gratifying.

What Is Macro Flow?

Macro flow is a comprehensive flow experience. It's marked by a distorted perception of time, a loss of self-consciousness, and total absorption into the task at hand. Everything unrelated to this task fades into the background and goes unnoticed. This is the state of mind that we've described throughout this book.

This is the quintessential flow experience. It's more intense and more fruitful than microflow. But all flow preconditions must be met.

Capitalize on All Flow Variants

To summarize, the flow experience is unlike a light switch that's either on or off. Gradients lie across a broad spectrum. The takeaway is that we can utilize flow wherever it occurs on this spectrum.

We can still take advantage of microflow if circumstances preclude us from enjoying a full-blown flow experience. And while our level of immersion and engagement isn't quite as deep during microflow, the experience can yield some of our most creative, fertile, and personally gratifying work.

HOW TO LENGTHEN A FLOW STATE

∽

Opinions vary regarding how long it is possible to stay in the zone. Research has suggested that the brain can operate optimally for only 45 minutes. But this conclusion comes from a study done in 1979.[1] We've since learned a lot more about brain activity during flow states.[2] Research now suggests that we can remain in flow for much longer periods. Today people from all walks of life report experiencing flow for hours.

Unfortunately, while we have the *ability* to stay in a flow state for extended periods, most of us let the opportunity slip through our fingers. In 2013, McKinsey & Company reported on the results of a 10-year survey conducted among 5,000 executives. A small number of the executives reported spending as much as half of their time in flow.

However, most reported spending less than 10 percent of their time in such a state.[3]

Circumstances will sometimes inhibit and can even ruin our flow experience. For example, a desperate coworker might barge into our office despite knowing we're unavailable, shattering our focus. At home, a family member might have a medical emergency and require immediate attention. Such situations demand precedence.

But such situations are rare. Our flow experience is usually abbreviated or disrupted due to factors we can influence. Bearing this in mind, the following are several productive steps to help us stay in the zone once we've entered it.

Address Small, Distracting Tasks First

Throughout each day, our attention is pulled away by numerous small tasks. They accumulate, looming over us and nagging us to address them. For example, we receive emails and texts that require a response. We notice voicemails are pending, and they pique our curiosity. We know that documents are sitting on our desks that need to be filed.

We can trigger a flow state despite these items hanging over our heads. But they'll be a distraction. They'll siphon off our attentional resources. We can avoid this scenario by attending to these tasks before we get into flow. Respond to those emails and texts. Listen to those voicemails (and respond to them, if necessary). File those documents.

When our headspace is cleared of this clutter, we can more easily prolong our flow experience.

Intensify the Challenge

Recall that one of the preconditions of flow is a balance between the difficulty of the task or activity and our ability to complete it. We must feel challenged but remain confident that we can overcome the challenge.

Sometimes a task may be challenging at the outset, but it becomes easier as we do it. With time, it can even become boring to us.

For example, imagine that you have a new job that involves data entry. Initially, you feel challenged because you're focused on correctly entering data with minimal errors. As time passes, however, muscle memory develops, and the job becomes monotonous. The challenge evaporates, and the balance between it and your ability is thrown askew. This isn't conducive to flow.

We can counter this effect and reestablish the challenge/skill balance by increasing the task's difficulty. One method is gamification, which we discussed in *Step #7: Choose a Challenging (But Achievable) Task*. Another method is called tangential immersion. It proposes doing two tedious tasks simultaneously to keep our brains occupied.[4]

The nub is that rebalancing a task's challenge/skill ratio can help us stay in flow when our mind might otherwise wander due to boredom.

Listen to the Right Sounds

Many assume that silence is an ally to concentration and thus facilitates flow. While this may hold for some, it isn't universally applicable. Numerous studies have shown that the brain responds positively to certain sounds.

For example, researchers noted in 1993 that listening to Mozart improved spatial reasoning.[5] This has become known as the Mozart effect. Recent research has shown that listening to white noise can help us to sustain our focus while boosting our creativity.[6] Researchers have also investigated using binaural and monoaural beats and their effects on our attention and cognitive performance.[7]

Listening to select sounds can help us to extend our flow state of mind. But the effects of various sounds vary from person to person. This being the case, uncovering the ones that work for *you* will require experimentation.

For example, you might find that the Mozart effect harms your flow experience, while Bach's textures are an ideal companion during flow sessions. Or you may discover that white noise is distracting, while "pink noise," which uses lower-frequency sound waves, has the opposite effect.

Experiment with a wide array of sounds. Take notes. Use what works and scrap what doesn't.

Plan Ahead to Avoid Potential Distractions

Some distractions are unavoidable. You can't do anything about them and must use compensatory tactics to preserve your focus. For example, you may work in an area where coworkers constantly chat with each other. You may have to wear noise-canceling headphones if you can't reserve a conference room or other quiet space.

But many distractions that threaten to ruin our focus and push us out of flow *can* be avoided. We can plan and steer clear of them if we can anticipate them.

For example, we can silence our phones, block our internet access, and work in a room without a wall clock. If we have an office, we can close the door. If we work at home, we can tell our family to refrain from interrupting us for a specified period unless there's an emergency. To avoid distracting hunger pangs, we can eat a small meal filled with protein and healthy fat before we work. We can break down large tasks into smaller ones to avoid getting distracted by feeling overwhelmed.

By taking these and other preventative actions, we shield ourselves from the avoidable chaos that would otherwise disrupt us. Doing so allows us to become fully immersed over a longer period.

Gather Your "Tools" before You Start

You'll need specific tools to perform depending on the task or activity. These tools can be physical, such as reference books, paper files, and various pieces of equipment (e.g., your laptop, drafting kit, cooking utensils, etc.). Or they might be digital, such as cloud-stored files, note-taking software, or various apps used for reference, analysis, and calculation.

If we start to work without first assembling these resources, we'll need to stop working and obtain them later. Doing so will disrupt our flow experience. It may even ruin it if we can't find what we need.

By gathering our tools beforehand, we ensure that we have all of the resources we need. We can thus avoid interrupting our flow while searching for them later.

Sometimes you'll require a resource or tool that isn't readily available to you to complete a task or activity. In such cases, note what you need and move on. Come back to it later.

For example, when I write a book, I often need to refer to research done by behavioral scientists. When this occurs, rather than stop writing, I type "{XYZ}" before moving forward. Later, I search for that string of characters in my text and do investigative work to find the appropriate studies. This allows me to continue writing in flow without interruption.

Summing It Up

Prolonging a flow state isn't an issue when we have only a short period available to us. But when we're fortunate enough to have an extended period available, we can take simple steps to extend our flow experience. The benefits we stand to realize from a sustained flow state make the effort worthwhile.

1. Parasuraman, R. (1979). Memory Load and Event Rate Control Sensitivity Decrements in Sustained Attention. *Science, 205*(4409), 924–927. https://doi.org/10.1126/science.472714
2. Katahira, K., Yamazaki, Y., Yamaoka, C., Ozaki, H., Nakagawa, S., & Nagata, N. (2018). EEG Correlates of the Flow State: A Combination of Increased Frontal Theta and Moderate Frontocentral Alpha Rhythm in the Mental Arithmetic Task. *Frontiers in Psychology, 9*. https://doi.org/10.3389/fpsyg.2018.00300
3. *Increasing the 'meaning quotient' of work*. (2013, January 1). McKinsey & Company. https://www.mckinsey.com/capabilities/people-and-organizational-performance/our-insights/increasing-the-meaning-quotient-of-work
4. Research surrounding tangential immersion is relatively recent. Additional research is needed to determine how effective it is for extending a flow state of mind. It's worth watching this area as the body of research grows.
5. Rauscher, F. H., Shaw, G. R., & Ky, K. N. (1993). Music and spatial task performance. *Nature, 365*(6447), 611. https://doi.org/10.1038/365611a0
6. Awada, M., Becerik-Gerber, B., Lucas, G. M., & Roll, S. C. (2022). Cognitive performance, creativity and stress levels of neurotypical young adults under different white noise levels. *Scientific Reports, 12*(1). https://doi.org/10.1038/s41598-022-18862-w
7. Engelbregt, H., Meijburg, N., Schulten, M., Pogarell, O., & Deijen, J. B. (2019). The Effects of Binaural and Monoaural Beat Stimulation on Cognitive Functioning in Subjects with Different Levels of Emotionality. *Advances in Cognitive Psychology, 15*(3), 199–207. https://doi.org/10.5709/acp-0268-8

THE POTENTIAL DARK SIDE OF ACHIEVING FLOW

> Enjoyable activities that produce flow… can become addictive, at which point the self becomes captive of a certain kind of order, and is then unwilling to cope with the ambiguities of life.
>
> — MIHALY CSIKSZENTMIHALYI

Flow is typically discussed in the context of its benefits and rewards. And to be sure, these are many and valuable. Flow helps us be more productive, more creative, less stressed and anxious, and more gratified by our efforts. The benefits and rewards we experience when we practice flow regularly can even improve our quality of life.

But there's a dark side. It's rarely discussed, but worth our attention. While flow is often said to be an "optimal state of consciousness," it can lead to negative consequences if we're not wary.

When Flow Becomes Addictive

The link between flow and addiction isn't yet entirely understood. Researchers suspect that the flow experience releases several neurotransmitters, one of which is dopamine, the "feel good" chemical. The prevailing view is that flow exposes the brain to dopamine, which gives the individual a feeling of euphoria. The individual is motivated to experience this sensation again and again.

This compulsion is common in those who regularly engage in risky activities. Consider the gambling addict who experiences euphoria when they win at their favored games of chance. They continue to gamble, chasing that sensation and hoping to experience it again despite mounting losses.

Consider "adrenaline junkies." They experience a dopamine rush when participating in various dangerous activities, such as skydiving, rock climbing, and wingsuiting. When the activity ends, they undergo a comedown period. The high wears off. They're left with an intense craving to feel that sensation again (i.e., withdrawal).

This experience is common among addicts of every kind. The salient point here is that it may also occur in those who spend significant time in a flow state. This can lead to poor risk assessment and risky behavior.[1]

Lack of Situational Awareness

One of the most common characteristics of flow is that the world around us fades away as we focus on the task in front of us. We become unaware of what's happening nearby when in a deep flow state. Our attentional resources are entirely devoted to what we're doing, and consequently, our situational awareness declines. It's not uncommon for those experiencing flow to appear as though they're in a trance.

This lack of situational awareness can have negative consequences that range from minor to disastrous. For example, imagine that you're working in a flow state at your job. You fail to hear a coworker who is addressing you. This individual may feel you're ignoring them and become resentful.

Or imagine that you're working in a flow state at home. You're alone, and a fire starts in your kitchen. In this case, a lack of situational awareness can present tremendous danger.

How to Stay in Control

Staying in control while we're in a flow state involves self-awareness and self-management. Ironically, the more we experience flow, the greater the need for both. It's possible to become so accustomed to being in the zone that we become less vigilant about our emotional and behavioral tendencies while in that state.

We can avoid this problem by practicing mindfulness. At first, the two practices seem to be at odds. How can we remain mindful of ourselves and our surroundings while simultaneously experiencing the lack of awareness associated with flow? Research shows that while mindfulness appears to be incompatible with flow *absorption*, which occurs during the onset of flow, it seems to be complementary to flow *control*, which occurs while we're deep in flow.[2]

The research investigating the connection between mindfulness and flow remains limited. While we wait for this body of research to grow, we can practice a few rudimentary mindfulness exercises to improve our emotional and behavioral control. Here are a few simple routines:

- Walking meditation
- Active listening
- Mindful eating
- Silent sitting
- Box breathing

These exercises are easy, simple, and can be performed in a short period of time. They're a good place to start if you've never practiced mindfulness.

The Road Forward

Researchers continue to study the relationship between flow and its adverse effects. But evidence thus far shows there's unquestionably a dark side to the flow experience. Ignoring it only exposes us to a greater risk of its consequences.

We can make ourselves less susceptible to this risk by prioritizing and practicing emotional and behavioral self-regulation. There's a tremendous benefit to improving our self-awareness and self-control while at the same time training ourselves to trigger and make use of the flow experience. For this reason, I strongly recommend doing the simple mindfulness exercises noted above whenever time allows.

---

1. Schüler, J., & Nakamura, J. (2013). Does Flow Experience Lead to Risk? How and for Whom. *Applied Psychology: Health and Well-Being*, 5(3), 311–331. https://doi.org/10.1111/aphw.12012
2. Sheldon, K. M., Prentice, M., & Halusic, M. (2015). The Experiential Incompatibility of Mindfulness and Flow Absorption. *Social Psychological and Personality Science*, 6(3), 276–283. https://doi.org/10.1177/1948550614555028

PART V

BONUS SECTION: 10 SIMPLE ACTIVITIES TO PRACTICE GETTING INTO FLOW

∼

It's relatively easy to induce a flow state when conditions are perfect. A distraction-free environment is ideal. Getting sufficient sleep each night, working during our peak energy times, and tackling activities with the right challenge/skills balance is likewise important. But if we want to trigger flow at will, we need to hone the ability.

Like an athlete who trains to prepare their body for competition, we can train to prepare our mind to enter and stay in flow. This bonus section will help. Included are ten exercises designed to train our minds to be amenable to a flow experience.

You may feel tempted to skip these exercises. Resist that

temptation. Left to its own devices, the mind is naturally inclined to daydream, multitask, and worry. These tendencies are detrimental to flow. Doing the following exercises will help us counter and suppress them when it matters.

Let's get started.

ACTIVITY #1: READ LONG-FORM, NON-FICTION CONTENT SLOWLY

∽

Reading is somewhat of a lost art these days. An astounding percentage of people choose not to read even a single book a year.[1] And while many folks start to read articles online, most choose not to finish them.[2]

We tend to skim rather than read. Our eyes drift across paragraphs, looking for phrases or details that interest us at that particular moment. When we find them, they arrest our attention. We slow down. Otherwise, we keep scanning.

The internet has only compounded this tendency. The volume of content at our fingertips increases each year exponentially. Consequently, we skim and scan as a matter of necessity as much as convenience.

So this activity — reading long-form, non-fiction

content slowly — will likely take effort. It'll require us to slow down when we read. Rather than skimming through articles, racing from one to the next, we'll train our minds to truly absorb what we read.

We might discover that we *enjoy* reading in this manner more than we would have imagined.

LET'S DO IT!

First, find a resource that offers a reservoir of long-form, non-fiction content. Here are a few of my favorites:

- LongForm.com[3]
- LongReads.com
- Atavist.com
- EpicMagazine.com
- r/indepthstories[4]

Second, select an article that interests you. The longer the piece, the better. If possible, choose one accompanied by few, if any, images.

Third, find a quiet place to read the article you've chosen. This can include your home office, a nearby park, or even sitting in your car in a deserted parking lot.[5]

Fourth, set a timer. If you're unaccustomed to reading

long-form articles, it may be difficult to focus while reading for extended periods. This can be the case even if you're interested in the subject. Set the timer for 10 minutes. Extend your reading sessions as your focus develops.

Lastly, and this is arguably the most important step, concentrate on every word, sentence, and paragraph you read. Absorb them. Comprehend how they either support or detract from the article's core narrative.

Time required: 15 minutes to select an article and complete your first reading session.

---

1. Pew Research published survey results in 2016 showing that 27% of Americans did not read a book in the preceding twelve months.
   Perrin, A., & Perrin, A. (2020, May 30). *Book Reading 2016*. Pew Research Center: Internet, Science & Tech. https://www.pewresearch.org/internet/2016/09/01/book-reading-2016/
2. Slate published findings in 2013 showing that, on average, only five percent of readers who land on an article on the site finish reading it. While these findings are old, I suspect this trend continues today.
   Manjoo, F. (2013, June 6). *You Won't Finish This Article*. Slate Magazine. https://slate.com/technology/2013/06/how-people-read-online-why-you-wont-finish-this-article.html
3. Longform.com is no longer actively publishing content. But their massive archive of articles (10,000+ pieces) remains available.
4. This is a subreddit on Reddit where members post links to investigative journalism pieces.
5. This used to be one of my favorite places to read. It's surprisingly peaceful. But make sure the area is safe (e.g., the parking lot of a popular retail venue one hour before it opens).

ACTIVITY #2: BRAINSTORM AN OUT-OF-THE-BOX SOLUTION TO AN EXISTING PROBLEM

∽

When confronted with a familiar problem, we instinctively try to resolve it by doing what has worked for us in the past. For example, if we encounter heavy traffic on our usual route home from work, we use an alternate route that we've previously used successfully. If we fail to plan a meal for dinner, we get takeout from a reliable and favored restaurant.

This is a practical approach to problem-solving. It saves time, conserves our mental energy, and produces an acceptable solution.

When we run into an unfamiliar problem, we take a similar approach, at least initially. We consider tactics that we've used in the past. Do they apply to our present situation? If so, we try them first. If not, we brainstorm a solution using our creativity, expertise, insight, and any factual details we possess or can uncover.

Creativity plays a vital role in the flow experience. Indeed it shares a symbiotic relationship with flow. Csikszentmihalyi described flow as "the sense of having stepped out of the routines of everyday life into a different reality." We're more creative when we're in the zone.

Conversely, research also shows that thinking outside the box can help induce flow.[1] Humans are great at recognizing patterns in everyday life. And we tend to run on autopilot based on them. But when we brainstorm and apply *new* ideas to those patterns, we pave the path toward flow. Our focus becomes sharper. Our level of engagement increases. Our inhibitions and self-consciousness recede into the background. When this happens, we're often swept right into the zone.

With this in mind, we should strengthen our creativity "muscles." Here's a quick and fun exercise to help us do that.

LET'S DO IT!

THIS EXERCISE HAS TWO STEPS. First, think about a problem that you're currently dealing with. If you have no problems (lucky you!), recall one from your recent past. It can be big or small, consequential or trivial.

Second, brainstorm every possible solution to this problem. Don't censor yourself. Write down everything that comes to mind, no matter how zany or impractical. No one will see your list of solutions but you. And you can destroy it when we're done.

For example, suppose the problem you've identified involves a chatty coworker who frequently visits and ruins your focus. Your list of solutions might include the following:

- Post a sign that says, "Do not disturb!"
- Tell "Beth" (the chatty coworker) that you're in the zone and need to concentrate.
- Tell the boss that "Beth" needs more work.
- Ask another coworker to run interference by intercepting "Beth" whenever she approaches.
- Give "Beth" to-do items every time she visits to chat.
- Pretend you're on a conference call.
- Interject whenever "Beth" tries to say something. (She may find the experience of chatting with you so unrewarding that she stops visiting.)
- Be contrary. If "Beth" complains about something, be cheerful. If she's cheerful, be pessimistic and cynical.
- Tell jokes that you know will annoy "Beth."

- Keep saying, "I don't understand, Beth."

Some of these "solutions" are impractical and may lead to bigger issues. But the purpose of this exercise isn't to solve the problem. Instead, it's to improve our creative thinking.

And be honest, you had a bit of fun, right?

Time required: 10 minutes

---

1. Schutte, N. S., & Malouff, J. M. (2020). Connections between curiosity, flow and creativity. *Personality and Individual Differences, 152*, 109555. https://doi.org/10.1016/j.paid.2019.109555

ACTIVITY #3: PRACTICE A BREATHING ROUTINE TO SHARPEN YOUR FOCUS

~

Most of us take breathing for granted. I certainly did until a few years ago. At the time, I was feeling stressed and overwhelmed. So I closed my eyes and concentrated solely on inhaling and then exhaling. Full, deep breaths. Inhale, then exhale. In, then out.

I did this on a whim. I needed a way to disconnect from the pressure I was feeling. It turned out that this simple breathing routine was exactly what I needed at that moment. Less than a minute later, I felt relaxed and refocused.

I felt... *good*.

Of course, the circumstances that were causing me stress were still present. But I could attend to them in a calm rather than a frazzled state of mind. That made all the difference in the world.

That was the moment I discovered the benefits of performing breathing exercises. That epiphany may sound silly because breathing happens naturally. We do it without thinking about it. But breathing *purposefully* is an entirely different thing. It offers rewards that are otherwise inaccessible to us.

Numerous studies highlight the physiological and cognitive benefits of doing breathing exercises.[1][2][3][4] There's no need for us to dawdle on that research here. It's enough to know that deep breathing reduces our stress and makes us *less vulnerable* to it.

This secondary effect is noteworthy. It occurs because deep breathing helps us to regulate our emotions during stressful periods. No longer feeling overwhelmed, we become more attentive, aware, relaxed, and focused. This frame of mind makes us more receptive to a flow experience.

〜

LET'S DO IT!

〜

TRY THIS SIMPLE BREATHING ROUTINE. It only requires a few minutes. You can do it practically anywhere at any time.

Before we start, take a few normal breaths. If you're like most people, these breaths will be relatively shallow. Next, take a few slow, *deep* breaths. Let the air fill your lower belly.[5] Feel the difference?

Now, close your eyes and slowly breathe in through your nose. Count to five as you do so. Once you've inhaled fully, hold it. Count again to five. Then, exhale slowly through your mouth while counting to five.

Do this five times.

Now open your eyes. You'll almost certainly feel more relaxed, aware, and focused. And although it's difficult to notice initially, you're on the way toward developing an important ability: emotional management during difficult situations. This ability will make you less vulnerable to feeling overwhelmed and better able to concentrate going forward.

I recommend doing this breathing routine a few times each day. I do so myself and have found that the benefits greatly outweigh the minimal time and effort required.

Time required: 5 minutes

---

1. Zaccaro, A., Piarulli, A., Laurino, M., Garbella, E., Menicucci, D., Neri, B., & Gemignani, A. (2018). How Breath-Control Can Change Your Life: A Systematic Review on Psycho-Physiological Correlates of Slow Breathing. *Frontiers in Human Neuroscience, 12.* https://doi.org/10.3389/fnhum.2018.00353
2. Jerath, R., Crawford, M. W., Barnes, V. A., & Harden, K. (2015). Self-Regulation of Breathing as a Primary Treatment for

Anxiety. *Applied Psychophysiology and Biofeedback, 40*(2), 107–115. https://doi.org/10.1007/s10484-015-9279-8
3. Doll, A., Hölzel, B. K., Bratec, S. M., Boucard, C. C., Xie, X., Wohlschläger, A. M., & Sorg, C. (2016). Mindful attention to breath regulates emotions via increased amygdala–prefrontal cortex connectivity. *NeuroImage, 134,* 305–313. https://doi.org/10.1016/j.neuroimage.2016.03.041
4. Ma, X., Yue, Z. E. J., Gong, Z., Zhang, H., Duan, N. Y., Shi, Y., Wei, G., & Niu, X. (2017). The Effect of Diaphragmatic Breathing on Attention, Negative Affect and Stress in Healthy Adults. *Frontiers in Psychology, 8.* https://doi.org/10.3389/fpsyg.2017.00874
5. This is called diaphragmatic breathing.

ACTIVITY #4: MEDITATE FOR 10 MINUTES

∾

Meditation is often mistaken for breathwork, particularly by those unfamiliar with the former. But the two are very different.

Breathwork uses diverse breathing techniques to improve physical and mental well-being. Our body and mind benefit from the oxygen that floods into our bloodstream. As noted in the previous section, it helps relieve our stress, relaxes us, and improves our focus.

Meditation is the use of varied practices to produce cognitive benefits primarily. It not only relieves stress, relaxes us, and improves our focus, but it can also improve our sleep, build up our attention span, and help us to manage our emotions. Research even suggests that long-term meditators suffer less age-related cognitive decline.[1]

Meditation isn't an alternative to breathwork. The two

are complementary, and both offer unique rewards.

Most people think of meditation in its most clichéd form. They imagine someone sitting silently on a pillow, eyes closed, legs crossed, arms extended, and fingers touching. This individual might recite a mantra or vocalize a soft "hummmmm."

In reality, there are many types of meditation,[2] and some can be performed while doing other things. In the activity below, we're going to do walking meditation.

LET'S DO IT!

One of the great things about walking meditation is that it gives us a chance to move our bodies. In addition to the usual roster of cognitive benefits, we get some exercise. And let's be honest. Who doesn't enjoy taking a short, leisurely walk?

First, wear comfortable clothes. If you intend to do this outside, wear comfortable shoes, too. (You can do walking meditation indoors if you prefer.)

Before you start walking, stand still and take a few deep breaths. Pay attention to your body as you do this. Note how your feet, legs, abdomen, chest, arms, and neck feel. Ignore what's happening around you for now. Concentrate instead on the physical sensations you're experiencing.

Now, begin walking at an unhurried pace. Focus on each footstep. Note how your legs feel each time you lift them. Observe how your arms swing back and forth in sync with your steps. Pay attention to your breathing, gait, and posture. Does your body feel flexible or stiff?

As you continue to walk, expand your awareness beyond your body. Notice the cars that pass by, the trees or structures around you, and the sounds and scents in your surroundings. Notice other people in your vicinity.

Discern small details. What was the make and model of that car that just drove by? What was that pedestrian wearing? How many floors did that building have?

Stop whenever you'd like.

Walking meditation benefits us in two ways. First, it helps us detach ourselves from the sundry distractions that assail us during a typical day. Second, it trains our minds to focus. The better our focus, the easier it is to get in the zone at will.

It's also fun and relaxing, and many of us need more of that in our lives.

Time required: at least 10 minutes

---

1. Luders, E., Cherbuin, N., & Kurth, F. (2015). Forever Young(er): potential age-defying effects of long-term meditation on gray matter atrophy. *Frontiers in Psychology*, *5*. https://doi.org/10.3389/fpsyg.2014.01551
2. These include transcendental meditation, visualization meditation, guided meditation, and Vipassana meditation (to name a few).

ACTIVITY #5: CONDUCT AN ACTIVE LISTENING SESSION

Have you ever found your mind wandering while someone is speaking to you? You start to think of other things, such as work-related issues, errands you need to run, and what to eat for lunch. We may pretend to pay attention and even nod at appropriate times, but our attention is elsewhere.

All of us have experienced this. Unfortunately, poor listening carries many consequences that we seldom anticipate. It leads to misunderstandings and hurt feelings. It causes trust and intimacy to deteriorate as the speaker infers that we lack empathy. If they're passing along important information, it can result in our making bad decisions and costly mistakes.

Another penalty to poor listening is that it gradually erodes our ability to focus. Each time we allow our thoughts to drift while listening (i.e., pseudo-listening), we train ourselves to be susceptible to distractions. We reinforce a habit of inattentiveness and disengagement.

When the time comes for us to focus — for example, during a flow experience — we can't. We may be able to trigger flow, but we can't stay in that state of mind for long. We've trained our minds to be too easily distracted.

We must break this bad habit before taking full advantage of flow. The following activity will help us retrain and rebuild our listening and focusing "muscles."

LET'S DO IT!

You may be tempted to practice active listening while chatting with others. Most "experts" recommend doing so. I disagree with this advice, at least in the beginning. In my opinion, we should take greater care with those relationships. We shouldn't subject other folks to our training until we've developed a rudimentary level of skill.

So instead, choose a podcast or TED Talk. Ideally, select one that covers subject matter that lies outside your interests.[1]

Next, with a pen and pad of paper in front of you, set a timer for 60 seconds. Start the timer and play the presentation. Listen attentively to the speaker. Concentrate on their points.

When your timer sounds off, stop the presentation. Write down every point made by the speaker. If they told a story, write down the details. If they offered advice, note the specifics.

Repeat this process until you can recall everything said within the 60-second window. Then, set your timer for two minutes. Then, three minutes. And so on.

Once you can do this successfully for a 10-minute session, practice with people. This will entail verbalizing your interest, asking questions for clarification, and summarizing the other person's statements and ideas.

But for now, start with podcasts and TED Talks. The upside is that you can do it in privacy and at your convenience.

Time required: 10 minutes

---

1. It's easy to listen to someone speak about things we're interested in. To truly sharpen our active listening skills, we need to challenge ourselves.

ACTIVITY #6: PERFORM A MINDFULNESS DRILL

∽

The relationship between mindfulness and flow is a complex one. At first glance, they appear to be at odds with one another. The former increases our general awareness. The latter narrows our focus to increase our engagement in a specific task or activity at the cost of our awareness of the world around us.

Mindfulness and flow seem incompatible. How can we become *more* aware and *less* aware at the same time? Research suggests that mindfulness improves some facets of flow while simultaneously impairing others.

In 2015, a review of three studies found that mindfulness increased trait flow, defined as the ability to focus while working against the state of absorption.[1] In 2016, a study observing competitive cyclists found that mindfulness-based interventions used to combat anxiety and pessimism led to flow experiences.[2] In 2021, researchers noted that mindfulness could indeed facilitate flow since both involve increased engagement in the present moment.[3]

The jury is still out regarding the *extent* to which mindfulness supports flow. But so far, evidence suggests the two are connected and share a positive association.

Thanks to a large and growing body of research, we know that mindfulness offers numerous health benefits — both physical and mental. Given that it also facilitates flow, we have good reason to strive to be more mindful.

∼

LET'S DO IT!

∼

THIS ACTIVITY IS CALLED "FIVE SENSES." I didn't come up with this one, but whoever did so deserves a medal. It's fun, simple, relaxing, and convenient; it can be done practically anywhere and anytime. I like to run through it while visiting a local park, but you can perform it at home, at your workplace, or while walking.

Here's how it works:

First, notice everything you can *see* in your vicinity. This includes people, cars, buildings, and trees (and squirrels if you're at a park). Focus on small details, including those you might otherwise overlook. What types of clothes are passersby wearing? What makes and models of vehicles are driving past you?

Next, notice things you can *feel*. If you're sitting on a bench, note its solidity under you. If it's windy outside, note how it feels on your skin. If you're walking, pay attention to how your pants feel as they come into contact with your legs.

Now, notice things you can *hear*. At the park, you might hear children playing nearby. Sitting in your kitchen, you may hear the hum of your refrigerator. In your workplace, you'll likely hear coworkers talking on the phone, printers running, and staplers being used.

Then, notice things you can *smell*. If you're taking a walking break near lunchtime, you might smell food being prepared by nearby restaurants. If you're at home and your spouse walks by, you may catch a whiff of the shampoo they used. If someone is smoking nearby, you'll likely smell their cigarette smoke.

Finally, notice things you can *taste*. I like to close my eyes for this one as it helps me to focus. Pay attention to the flavor of the gum you're chewing. Take note of the flavor of the beverage you're drinking. Concentrate on your breath as you inhale and exhale.

This activity helps us to expand our awareness in the present moment. It also allows us to practice mindfulness when we have neither the time nor privacy to perform more formal exercises.

Time required: 5 minutes

1. Schutte, N. S., & Malouff, J. M. (2023). The connection between mindfulness and flow: A meta-analysis. *Personality and Individual Differences, 200*, 111871. https://doi.org/10.1016/j.paid.2022.111871
2. Scott-Hamilton, J., Schutte, N. S., & Brown, R. F. (2016). Effects of a Mindfulness Intervention on Sports-Anxiety, Pessimism, and Flow in Competitive Cyclists. *Applied Psychology: Health and Well-Being, 8*(1), 85–103. https://doi.org/10.1111/aphw.12063
3. Marty-Dugas, J., Smith, A. C., & Smilek, D. (2021). Focus on your breath: Can mindfulness facilitate the experience of flow? *Psychology of Consciousness*. https://doi.org/10.1037/cns0000251

ACTIVITY #7: DO YOUR FAVORITE PHYSICAL ACTIVITY WITH HYPERFOCUS

∼

We rely heavily on muscle memory when we perform everyday activities. We carry out the applicable motor skills without thinking much about them. As we repeat an action, neural pathways are created in our brains. The more frequently we take a particular action, the stronger the attendant pathways grow. Eventually, we can perform it on autopilot.

For example, recall when you learned to ride a bicycle. The activity was unfamiliar to you, and you likely found it difficult to do well your first time. But each attempt became easier. Each time you climbed onto your bicycle, grabbed the handlebars, and started pedaling, you had less difficulty. Eventually, you could do it without any trouble at all.

Today, you can ride a bicycle on autopilot. You hardly

need to think about how to do it. That's your muscle memory at work.

The neural pathways created while learning an activity help facilitate a flow experience once you're adept at the activity. At that point, you no longer need to think it through. You can rely on muscle memory. This frees you to get in the zone and lose yourself in what you're doing.

But arriving at that point requires that we perform the activity properly. It's possible to do something incorrectly, over and over, and form neural pathways that reinforce our mistakes. In that case, muscle memory can actually *hamper* our ability to induce flow and negatively impact our performance once we do so.

∽

LET'S DO IT!

∽

THIS ACTIVITY IS similar to the "Five Senses" mindfulness drill we performed in the previous section. But rather than focusing on sight, touch, sound, smell, and taste, we'll focus on our individual actions while doing an activity.

First, select a physical activity you'd like to perform in a flow state. This might be a particular sport, a specific hobby, or something you do that's related to your job.

Next, perform this activity while paying attention to

every action it involves. Note whether you're inclined to do them on autopilot. Have you developed muscle memory?

At each step, ask yourself whether you're taking action correctly. If you aren't, stop. You'll need to adjust in order to form the right neural pathways and build muscle memory that facilitates flow.

For example, suppose you want to play basketball in a flow state. You'll need to pay close attention to how you handle the ball, how you pass it to your teammates, and how you shoot. You'll also need to note how you move among your teammates and those on the opposing team.

A lot of "moving parts" are involved with being a proficient basketball player. Executing any of them improperly will erode your confidence, increase your stress, and obstruct your ability to get in the zone. Bad habits must be corrected.

Our goal here is to identify stumbling blocks, no matter how small, that influence how we perform our favorite activity. Once we identify them, we can make adjustments, improving our ability to trigger and maintain flow for this activity.

Time required: 15 minutes

ACTIVITY #8: ENJOY A ONE-HOUR DIGITAL DETOX

∾

The internet is a remarkably handy tool. We use it for research, education, communication, and file management. We go online to shop, pay our bills, make travel plans, and manage our money. We interact with friends and loved ones who live far away from us. When we use the internet with purpose and restraint, it's a valuable resource.

Our phones are similarly valuable. In addition to the above uses, it puts countless beneficial apps at our fingertips. These apps can help us increase our productivity, track and manage our time, and mark our progress while developing good habits.

But these tools are a double-edged sword. As helpful as they are, they pose significant adverse effects. For example, researchers suspect that the internet might influence how our brains function, harming our attention spans and memory processes.[1] Spending too much time online can even lead to internet addiction.[2] Studies suggest that our phones impose similar consequences.[3] And like the internet, excessive use can lead to smartphone addiction.[4] This often leads to feelings of anxiety, social isolation, depression, and even paranoia.[5]

These effects are the bane of flow. They can prevent us from experiencing flow altogether.

Most of us can't and shouldn't abandon our digital lives. Doing so would be impractical. Foolish, even. These tools, when we use them properly, arguably improve our quality of life.

That said, we can temper our use.

LET'S DO IT!

THIS ACTIVITY IS the simplest of them all. You may also find it the most enjoyable. We're going to do a 60-minute digital detox.

First, review your schedule. Choose a time when you can be away from your computer, phone, and other devices for one hour. We don't want anything to interfere with this activity.

Turn off your phone. Put it somewhere out of sight so you won't be tempted to use it.

Walk away from your computer. It's not enough to turn off your internet connection. We want to refrain from looking at the screen.

Don't turn on your TV. Don't substitute one screen for another.

Avoid driving. Unless you drive an older model, your vehicle is probably loaded with electronics, such as an entertainment system and various sensors that light up the dashboard.

Spend the next hour doing anything you want, as long as it doesn't involve your phone and other gadgets. For example, journal, read, go for a walk, clean your house, wash your car, or tend to your garden.

Enjoy the electronic-free time. And don't be surprised if you feel more relaxed, focused, confident, and creative while doing so.

Time required: 60 minutes

---

1. Firth, J., Torous, J., Stubbs, B., Firth, J., Steiner, G. Z., Yang, L., Alvarez-Jimenez, M., Gleeson, J., Vancampfort, D., Armitage, C. J., & Sarris, J. (2019). The "online brain": how the Internet may be changing our cognition. *World Psychiatry, 18*(2), 119–129. https://doi.org/10.1002/wps.20617
2. Kumar, M., & Mondal, A. (2018). A study on Internet addiction and its relation to psychopathology and self-esteem among college students. *Industrial Psychiatry Journal, 27*(1), 61. https://doi.org/10.4103/ipj.ipj_61_17

3. Small, G. W., Lee, J., Kaufman, A., Jalil, J., Siddarth, P., Gaddipati, H., Moody, T. D., & Bookheimer, S. Y. (2020b). Brain health consequences of digital technology use. *Dialogues in Clinical Neuroscience*, *22*(2), 179–187. https://doi.org/10.31887/dcns.2020.22.2/gsmall
4. Ratan, Z. A., Parrish, A., Zaman, S. B., Alotaibi, M. H., & Hosseinzadeh, H. (2021). Smartphone Addiction and Associated Health Outcomes in Adult Populations: A Systematic Review. *International Journal of Environmental Research and Public Health*, *18*(22), 12257. https://doi.org/10.3390/ijerph182212257
5. Guo, W., Tao, Y., Li, X., Lin, X., Meng, Y., Yang, X., Wang, H., Zhang, Y., Tang, W., Wang, Q., Deng, W., Zhao, L., Ma, X., Li, M., Chen, T., Xu, J., Li, J., Hao, W., Lee, S., . . . Li, T. (2020). Associations of Internet Addiction Severity With Psychopathology, Serious Mental Illness, and Suicidality: Large-Sample Cross-Sectional Study. *Journal of Medical Internet Research*, *22*(8), e17560. https://doi.org/10.2196/17560

ACTIVITY #9: QUESTION YOURSELF TO IDENTIFY FLOW BLOCKAGES

∽

Resistance to flow can spring from many sources. Those that originate and reside in our minds are among the most insidious. We're often unaware of them and thus unable to address them. They lie in the background, working against our intentions without our notice.

I'll give you an example from my own life. In my youth, I was a competitive swimmer. I loved the sport and was passionate about it — in the beginning. But as I grew older, other matters became more important to me. It became increasingly difficult for me to get in the zone during practice and competitions. At that stage of my life, I lacked the awareness to understand why I couldn't find my flow.

I spent years in this strange mental purgatory of doing something I once loved but no longer did. I couldn't reconcile my steadily declining performance, and my frustration grew.

Eventually, I figured it out. I asked myself frank questions regarding my feelings toward the sport and discovered I was apathetic. My brain had become so accustomed to loving the sport in the past that I felt compelled to love it in the present. This was an epiphany for me. I quit competitive swimming and immediately felt better.

At the time, I was also learning to play the guitar. But I was having trouble getting in the zone there, as well. That was because I was dividing my emotional and attentional resources. Quitting competitive swimming freed up those resources. Devoting them to playing the guitar, something I *actually* wanted to do, flow came easier.

Internal resistance to flow is often hard to identify. Self-questioning is a potent way for us to uncover it. Once it's exposed, we can address it constructively.

LET'S DO IT!

To use a plumbing euphemism, this activity will help to unclog our mental pipes. It gives us an opportunity to be introspective and ultimately flush the cognitive and emotional detritus that might otherwise block our flow.

We're going to ask ourselves three candid questions:

1. Why is this activity important to me?
2. What do I want to achieve by doing this activity?
3. How will I feel if I achieve my goal?

There are, of course, dozens of other questions that we can ask. But these three questions drive to the heart of the matter quickly.

We may discover that the activity we assume is important isn't any longer to us (or perhaps never was). We might learn that we're genuinely passionate about it, but our purpose for doing it is unclear. We might realize that achieving our goal won't satisfy us as we imagined.

This activity gives us clarity. It opens up the mental pipes and clears the way for us to experience flow — here or elsewhere. One way or the other, it helps us decide whether we should do what we intend to do.

(No more euphemisms. I promise.)

Time required: 15 minutes

ACTIVITY #10: SUMMARIZE CONTENT THAT YOU HAVE READ

∼

At the beginning of this bonus section, I mentioned that reading has become a lost art. While true, that's imprecise. It's more accurate to say that we rarely read *carefully*. We skim and scan. We glance through articles, reports, and even entire books, looking for details that we consider interesting or relevant at that moment.

This practice serves a purpose. Our lives are busy, and skimming helps us to optimize our time. Often, it's enough to get a general impression of an author's ideas. If we're in a rush, why waste our precious time on unnecessary details?

The problem is that we can become so accustomed to skim reading that our "deep reading" processes atrophy. These include deductive reasoning, critical analysis, and the ability to reflect, evaluate, and even empathize with the author. As these processes erode, we become more easily distracted. We find focusing more difficult, which impedes our ability to induce flow.

I'm sure you can relate to this. How many times have you skimmed an article only to realize, after reaching its end, that you couldn't recall the author's main points? If the article contained important details, you might have been forced to reread it.

Everyone has experienced this issue. Some of us experience it over and over throughout the day. It harms our productivity. It causes us to mismanage and squander our attentional resources. And it obstructs our flow.

So let's rebuild our deep reading skills. In the process, we'll improve our focus, insulating ourselves from the sundry distractions constantly trying to hijack our attention.

∾

LET'S DO IT!

∾

FOR THIS ACTIVITY, grab a few magazines that cover a variety of subject matter. Avoid content about current events and celebrities. Instead, opt for magazines that offer more insightful, thoughtful, or provocative content. Examples include *Scientific American*, *The New Yorker*, and *Psychology Today*.

I recommend reading magazines you can hold in your hands rather than reading them online. The latter experience poses too many distractions.

Choose a short article from one of the magazines in front of you (e.g., fewer than 1,000 words). Read it through to its end. Don't take notes. Don't reread passages. Don't pause to commit details to memory. Keep moving forward.

Once you've finished reading the article, summarize it. Use no more than three sentences. You can do this in writing or orally. Don't refer back to the article yet.

After you've written (or verbalized) your summary, check it for accuracy. Does it capture the author's main points or ideas? Does it align with the article's structure? If so, repeat this exercise with a longer piece (e.g., 2,000 words). If not, repeat it with a shorter one.

Deep reading helps us to improve our awareness and deepen our focus. It trains our minds to fully immerse in what we're reading, insulating us from the distractions and chaos surrounding us.

This is excellent practice for learning to trigger a flow state.

Time required: 25 minutes

FINAL THOUGHTS ON THE ART OF FINDING FLOW

∼

Flow is too often discussed as an enigma. Most people, even those who experience it regularly, assume it occurs by happenstance. They enjoy it whenever it happens but feel they have minimal control over it.

The truth is that you can induce flow at any time. It's primarily a matter of training. Once the correct building blocks are in place, you're in control. You can trigger this optimal state of mind at will and experience greater creativity, effortless concentration, and total engagement. In this state, you'll not only do your best work but also feel the most connected to it.

The *Art of Finding FLOW* is both a user's manual and a workshop. It provides a step-by-step action plan for learning to trigger flow and offers specially designed exercises along the way.

The upside is that you now have the tools you need to get in the zone at any time that suits you. Whether you're a musician, athlete, corporate manager, freelancer, stay-at-home parent, or some combination thereof, you now possess the drivers that lead to flow.

But it takes practice and requires awareness. Inducing this state of consciousness calls for select preconditions that lead to — and affect the quality of — your flow experience.

This book puts everything at your fingertips. To that end, I encourage you to do the exercises and activities once and return to them as needed. Like any skill, the ability to get in the zone strengthens with use and atrophies through nonuse. Maintaining proficiency requires exercising certain "muscles," like a professional runner who lifts weights to stay in top form.

Don't let this book gather dust (or digital dust if you own the ebook). Put it to use in a manner that best suits you. Reread certain sections to remind yourself of critical points and helpful tactics. Revisit select chapters to ensure you're about to take purposeful, effective action.

This is your vehicle, and the keys are in your hands. You decide your destination. It's my sincere hope that you enjoy the ride.

DID YOU ENJOY READING THE ART OF FINDING FLOW?

∽

Thank you for spending your time with me in this book. It means a lot to me, and I appreciate it. I hope you found the experience rewarding.

If you enjoyed reading *The Art of Finding FLOW* and found it helpful, would you mind doing me a small favor? Would you leave a short review for the book on Amazon? A sentence or two about something you liked would mean the world to me.

I could tell people to read the book until I'm blue, but *your* words will have a much greater impact. Potential readers want to hear from folks like yourself who have read the book.

One last note: I plan to write several more books like this one. I intend to release them at a steep discount for a limited time; you'll be able to grab each one for less than $1.

If you'd like to be notified when these books are released, and take advantage of the discounted price, be sure to join my mailing list. You'll immediately receive my 40-page PDF ebook titled *Catapult Your Productivity! The Top 10 Habits You Must Develop to Get More Things Done*.

You can join my list at the following address:

http://artofproductivity.com/free-gift/

I'll also send you my best productivity, time management, and self-development advice via my email newsletter. You'll receive tips and tactics on beating procrastination, creating morning routines, avoiding burnout, and developing razor-sharp focus, along with many other productivity hacks!

If you have questions or would like to share a tip, technique, or mind hack that has made a positive difference in your life, please feel free to reach out to me at damon@artofproductivity.com. I'd love to hear about it!

Until next time,

Damon Zahariades
http://artofproductivity.com

ABOUT THE AUTHOR

Damon Zahariades is a corporate refugee who endured years of unnecessary meetings, drive-by chats with coworkers, and a distraction-laden work environment before striking out on his own. Today, in addition to writing a growing catalog of time management and productivity books, he's the showrunner for the productivity blog <u>ArtofProductivity.com</u>.

In his spare time, he enjoys playing chess, poker, and the occasional video game with friends. And he continues to promise himself that he'll start playing the guitar again.

Damon lives in Southern California with his beautiful, supportive wife and their affectionate, quirky, and sometimes mischievous dog. He's looking wistfully at his 50th birthday in the rearview mirror.

OTHER BOOKS BY DAMON ZAHARIADES

The Mental Toughness Handbook

The Procrastination Cure

To-Do List Formula

The Time Management Solution

80/20 Your Life!

The Time Chunking Method

How to Make Better Decisions

The Art of Living Well series

The Art Of Saying NO

The Art of Letting GO

The Art of Finding FLOW

The 30-Day Productivity Boost series

The 30-Day Productivity Plan - VOLUME I

The 30-Day Productivity Plan - VOLUME II

Self-Help Books for Busy People series

Small Habits Revolution

The Joy Of Imperfection

The P.R.I.M.E.R. Goal Setting Method

Improve Your Focus and Mental Discipline series

Fast Focus

Morning Makeover

Digital Detox

Visit ArtofProductivity.com for a complete list of titles and summaries. All titles are available for purchase at ArtofProductivity.com/Amazon.

Printed in Great Britain
by Amazon